57 HOT BUSINESS MARKETING STRATEGIES

57 Hot Business Marketing Strategies

Offline And Online Marketing Techniques, Tips And Tricks From Successful Entrepreneurs

TOM CORSON-KNOWLES

Copyright © 2012, 2014, 2016
by Tom Corson-Knowles.

All Right Reserved.

Arial & Cambria fonts used with permission from Microsoft.

No part of this publication may be reproduced, distributed, or transmitted in any form or by any means, including photocopying, recording, or other electronic or mechanical methods, or by any information storage and retrieval system without the prior written permission of the publisher, except in the case of very brief quotations embodied in critical reviews and certain other noncommercial uses permitted by copyright law.

Get Tom's free newsletter for more marketing tips at:

www.BlogBusinessSchool.com

Published by TCK Publishing

www.TCKPublishing.com

Earnings Disclaimer

When addressing financial matters in any of our books, sites, videos, newsletters or other content, we've taken every effort to ensure we accurately represent our products and services and their ability to improve your life or grow your business. However, there is no guarantee that you will get any results or earn any money using any of our ideas, tools, strategies or recommendations, and we do not purport any "get rich schemes" in any of our content. Nothing in this book is a promise or guarantee of earnings. Your level of success in attaining similar results is dependent upon a number of factors including your skill, knowledge, ability, dedication, business savvy, network, and financial situation, to name a few. Because these factors differ according to individuals, we cannot and do not guarantee your success, income level, or ability to earn revenue. You alone are responsible for your actions and results in life and business. Any forward-looking statements outlined in this book or on our Sites are simply our opinion and thus are not guarantees or promises for actual performance. It should be clear to you that by law we make no guarantees that you will achieve any results from our ideas or models presented in this book or on our Sites, and we offer no professional legal, medical, psychological or financial advice.

Contents

Why I Wrote This Book xi
Introduction xiii
Part 1 Online Marketing 1
   1. Facebook 3
   2. YouTube 6
   3. Twitter 8
   4. LinkedIN 10
   5. Pinterest 14
   6. Niche Forums 16
   7. Affiliates 18
   8. Online Joint Venture Partners 20
   9. Create a Podcast or Web TV Show 22
   10. Blogging 25

11. Guest Blogging 27
12. eBook Publishing and Marketing 41
13. Pay-Per-Click Ads 44
14. Squidoo 46
15. Video Marketing 48
16. Search Engine Optimization 50
17. Offer A Free Report 52
18. Article Writing 55
19. Create a Song 56
20. Create Something Outrageous 58
21. Create a Membership Site or Program 60
22. Blogger Product Reviews 63
23. Coupon Sites 65
24. MeetUp.com 68

Part 2 Offline Marketing 71

25. Business Cards 72
26. Write For Newspapers and Publications 76
27. Volunteer 78
28. Join the SBA Small Business Mentoring
    Program 80
29. Write A Book 82
30. Phone Calls 84
31. Customer Marketing 88

32. Hosting An Event 91
33. Create A Branded Product 93
34. Public Speaking... 97
35. Turning Cold Calls Into Warm Calls.......................... 100
36. Find Your Best Buyers 103
37. Referral Program 106
38. Networking.. 108
39. Samples 111
40. Be Entertaining.. 113
41. Retail Partnerships 116
42. Press Releases.. 118
43. Car Detailing and Logos 122
44. Coupons and Gift Vouchers 124
45. Local Physical Marketing... 127
46. Donating Books.. 129
47. Gift Bags 131
47. Fundraising For Charity... 134
48. Write a Thank You Note... 137
49. Community Classes.. 140
50. Postcards For Local Businesses................................ 142
51. Create A Controversial Policy................................... 144
52. Create A Documentary 146
53. Direct Mail... 148

54. Flyers 151
55. Handing Out Branded Apparel 153
56. Create A Business Marketing Research
    Project 154
57. Radio and Media Appearances 159
Bonus Marketing Tips **161**
Promoting Your Website Offline 162
Tracking Phone Calls From Your Website 164
Bonus Sales Tip 167
Special Facebook Group 171
Free Blogging for Business Training 172
Connect With The Author 173
About The Author 175
Other Books By Tom Corson-Knowles 177
Index 179

WHY I WROTE THIS BOOK

OVER 70% OF Americans say they want to start a business... some day.

Many never do. If you've started a business or are considering starting one, I believe you deserve to have access to the world's greatest marketing strategies. I wrote this book to help entrepreneurs like you take their business to the next level.

For me, I was born to be in business. I don't know why or how, I just know that ever since I was young I never wanted to spend my life working for someone else. I wanted to do my own thing. I wanted to make a difference. I wanted to help others live a better life. I wanted to live life on my own terms. Being an entrepreneur has allowed me to do just that.

I started my first business at age 13, manufacturing SAD lamps out of my father's garage. It was a good business for a 13-year-old, but I quickly grew tired of manual labor. So I quit that business, and I started several other small ventures until age 19 when I decided to start a business selling a nutritional supplement on commissions. It was the best decision I've ever made!

I soon learned that selling is great, but marketing is even better! When you go out and sell products, you have to be there to convince your customers to buy. But when you use best practices in marketing yourself and your business, customers come find you asking to buy! It makes your job a lot easier, it takes less time and work, and the rewards can be far more profitable because you can scale up your marketing faster than you scale up your sales force.

In my seven years of experience in direct selling and online marketing, I've attended more than a hundred business seminars and workshops, read over 1,000 books on business and marketing, and tested literally thousands of different marketing strategies and tactics.

In this book, I won't share with you every single one of those marketing techniques and strategies I tested. I'm only going to share with you *the best and most effective* marketing strategies I've used to grow my own businesses.

All you have to do is read and apply this information to grow your business, transform your life and increase your income.

This book will help you grow your business!

Introduction

ARE YOU AS excited about marketing as I am?

You should be!

Marketing is the heartbeat of any business. Without marketing there are no sales. Without sales there are no profits. Without profits there is no business!

At least 80% of your business activity should be focused on marketing. Yes, building a great product is important. Yes, delivering your product with great customer service is important. The truth is there are many aspects of business that you must master to be successful. There is no one secret to success! And there is no one secret to marketing either. That's why I'm sharing 57 of my best marketing strategies with you – because just one strategy won't cut it!

You won't need to use all 57 of these strategies to grow your business. Maybe just a half dozen of these strategies, when applied diligently, can double, triple, or quadruple your business in just a few short months or years.

You must realize that there is no part of business that can ever make up for a lack of good marketing. It doesn't matter how good your product is if no one knows about it. Marketing is what builds great businesses and great companies. Marketing is what connects customers with wonderful products and services that solve their problems. I'm assuming you already have a wonderful product or service (or soon will). Let this book show you how to help more customers with your wonderful product or service!

I'm passionate about marketing, and teaching entrepreneurs like you how to market their businesses better.

Here's to your success!

Part 1

Online Marketing

First, we'll cover online marketing strategies and resources. Most of these are absolutely free to use.

1. FACEBOOK

FACEBOOK IS NOW the biggest website in the world. It's even bigger than Google! And Facebook has a specific platform for businesses to promote and market themselves using Facebook Fan Pages.

It's completely free to start a Facebook Fan Page, and I highly recommend you do.

I get dozens of qualified leads every month from my Facebook Fan Pages[1] and you can too!

All you have to do is get started, study the platform and implement best practices when marketing on Facebook. I've also written a detailed book on Facebook marketing and advertising[2] that will walk

---

[1] https://www.faceBook.com/OnlineInternetMarketingHelp
[2] http://www.amazon.com/Facebook-Business-Owners-Marketing-Businesses-eBook/dp/B009PPCPUE

you through every single aspect of marketing your business on Facebook.

For now, if you don't have a fan page, create one! If you already have a fan page created, make sure you're posting high quality, relevant content every single day.

Most businesses treat Facebook and other social media sites as tools for "selling." But marketing is *not* sales. Marketing leads to sales. Before you can sell customers, you must attract their attention and get their interest. Use Facebook as a platform for attracting attention and getting interest – *not as a platform for selling.*

When you do this, you will start to get more leads from Facebook. Then, once you've built a relationship and attracted leads, you can begin to move those leads through your sales process.

If you start by trying to sell on social media, you won't make any sales. If you start with attracting the attention of your target customers and peak their interest enough to have them reach out and contact you, subscribe to your email list, or visit your website, your sales will grow.

One great way to attract attention and gain the interest of your target customers is to start sharing relevant, useful and helpful educational information on your page. Let's say you run a car repair shop, for example. You could post helpful tips on car maintenance, create a video about why car owners should get a regular oil change, or post the answer to a frequently asked question. This helpful content will 1) attract attention from your target customers, 2) add value to your target customers, 3) brand you or your company as the expert in your field, and 4) keep you top-of-mind in your field so that when your customers need car repairs, they first think of you and not your competitors.

When you're writing a post on your Facebook fan page, stop and ask yourself:

Is this post going to attract the attention of my target customer?

Will this post add value and help my target customer?

If the answer is yes, post it! If not, try to rewrite your post so that it will attract more attention and add more value to your customers.

~ ACTION STEP ~

Just go to Facebook.com/pages/create and create your Facebook Fan Page today. Then just start posting unique, fun, interesting and educational information for your fans and followers and post special offers every now and then and watch the sales come in.

2. YouTube

YOUTUBE IS THE biggest video hosting website in the world, and it's the second largest search engine in the world after Google.

If you've ever created a video for your business, I highly recommend uploading it to YouTube with a link in the description to your website. You can also create more videos just for marketing your business online.

You don't have to be a professional videographer to use YouTube to grow your business. Most ultra-successful YouTubers just started out with very simple equipment like a Flip camera, iPhone, or a simple webcam.

A quick and easy way to get started is just to use your iPhone or smartphone camera to record a video of you talking. You can explain your products or services or just answer common customer questions and post the videos on YouTube.

Online video is the fastest growing segment of advertising because it works so well in turning prospects into customers. Online video is booming right now, and if you're not taking advantage of it, you're missing out.

~ ACTION STEP ~

Sign up for an account at YouTube.com if you don't have one.

Then write down the 10 most commonly asked questions you get from customers and answer each one in a 1-5 minute video. Just record yourself speaking the answers to the qustions using an iPhone or other smartphone camera, tablet or webcam and upload the videos to your YouTube channel.

3. Twitter

TWITTER IS ONE of those booming websites which most small business owners "just don't get." That's okay! You don't have to "get it" to profit from it.

Why does every Fortune 500 company have a team of people dedicated to managing their Twitter account? Because being active on Twitter is a great way to attract new customers and keep in touch with your existing customers.

Twitter is an incredible way to connect with your current customers and prospects and help answer questions and solve problems for potential customers while they're making a purchasing decision. It's also a great way to get referrals organically!

3. TWITTER

> ### ~ ACTION STEP ~
>
> Create a new Twitter account if you don't have one already at Twitter.com and start tweeting!
>
> You can read my free report *How To Make Money With Twitter* to learn how to systemize your Twitter marketing to bring in hundreds of new leads every months for your business for less than $50.
>
> **http://www.blogbusinessschool.com/ how-to-make-money-with-twitter**

4. LinkedIN

LINKEDIN IS THE premier social network for highly paid professionals, CEOs and entrepreneurs. If you sell to other entrepreneurs or run B2B business, LinkedIN can help you find and connect with those key people and prospects who could double or triple your business. You can turn what used to be cold calls into warm calls using LinkedIN's amazing platform to start connecting with the best possible prospects for your business.

On LinkedIN, you can get new leads for your business in numerous ways. First of all, make sure to fill out your profile completely with your website and information about what you do and how you help your customers.

Next, you can join groups for your industry or customer's industry and share valuable information, answer questions and network with clients and referral partners.

Next, you can search for the people you want to connect with who would be good business partners or clients for you. For example, if you have a list of the top companies that could be great clients for your business, search for those companies on LinkedIN and connect with the key people in that company to start the sales process.

You can also participate in LinkedIN's Questions and answer questions related to your field of expertise. Other users then vote on the usefulness and helpfulness of your answers which gives great social proof of your knowledge and expertise.

Another option you have on LinkedIN for growing your business is advertising.

LinkedIN Advertising Case Study

"LinkedIN has a been a tremendous resource in building Koyal's recognition and our network of brand ambassadors worldwide. Koyal is an active member of 4 groups in particular that we have used to build up our clientele as well showcase new product line releases.

LinkedIn offers $50 in free advertising several times a year, and we decided to test the waters earlier this year. We were able to connect with wedding and event professional and planners through these ads, which we target to our four main professional groups:

- Event Planning & Event Management - the 1st Group for Event Professionals
- Event Planning Professionals
- Wedding Market
- Wedding Professionals Networking Group

By directing our advertising towards these groups, we have been able to hone our new product and initiatives messages directly at our target demographic groups of wedding and event planners, coordinators and brides themselves.

LinkedIN has also been a tremendous hiring resource for Koyal, as we have been able to vet candidates based on past experience, strengths and skills directly from the platform. We have been able to target our search within Southern California's Orange County and Inland Empire talent pools, which has led to tremendous success on our hiring front. In addition, we have been able to monitor the hirings of our competitors in order to spot trends in where they will be allocating resources for the short and long-term."

Shreyans Parekh
KoyalWholesale.com

> **~ ACTION STEP ~**
>
> If you're not on LinkedIN yet, sign up for a new account at:
>
> **www.LinkedIN.com**
>
> Add your email contacts as connections, join some relevant groups for your industry and start connecting with the key influencers and prospects in your target market.

5. Pinterest

PINTEREST IS HUGE. In 2013, it became the fastest growing website in the world and by 2015 it had amassed 176 million registered users. And it's all about pictures.

I highly recommend using Pinterest, especially if you are in retail, clothing, fashion, jewelery or any business with physical products that people like to look at. You can post pictures of your products on Pinterest (with price tags) and watch the sales roll in!

Pinterest's biggest user demographic is women, so Pinterest is a great marketing platform especially if your business sells primarily to women.

If you're not sure what to post on Pinterest, check out Pinerly[3] as a good tool to help you get started. It's a great resource that will make it super easy to find images to post and even gives you tracking and analytics for your pins.

> **~ ACTION STEP ~**
> If you don't have an account yet, sign up for one at:
> **www.Pinterest.com**

---

[3] http://www.pinerly.com/i/7A719

6. Niche Forums

DID YOU KNOW there are literally hundreds of online forums where your customers and potential customers go to learn, share and connect with others in your industry?

If you're not on these forums then you're missing out on the chance to connect with these customers and prospects and become known as an expert in your field.

For example, if you're a gardening expert and sell gardening books, DVDs or equipment, I would highly recommend joining several of the biggest gardening forums. Once you've joined, you can start increasing your influence by answering questions, building relationships and helping people out.

6. NICHE FORUMS

How does posting on forums pay off?

In forums you can post a link in your signature to your website with some words that describe what you do and what you offer. People will naturally find your posts through the forum and click your link to learn more.

People would rather buy from someone who's helpful in a forum than some random website they have no connection with!

Furthermore, many of the best forum posts get shared with others, printed out, linked back to in other forum posts and blogs, and so their effect and influence snowballs over time. A single great forum post in your field could continue to drive new prospects and customers your way for years and years to come.

~ ACTION STEP ~

Search Google for large forums in your niche and join 1 or 2 of the biggest forums.
Start posting valuable information and see how the forum responds. Each forum is totally different with different rules and members so what may work in one forum might not work in another.
In general, if you provide useful information for people they will respond very positively.

7. Affiliates

IF YOU DON'T have affiliates for your business I highly recommend considering offering this option to help your promotional partners earn more money while you grow your business.

Affiliate marketing doesn't work in every business but it works incredibly well in any online business that sells digital content (such as eBooks, worksheets, software, video trainings, webinars, etc.). Affiliate marketing also works great with physical products sold online. Netflix, Drugstore.com, and Amazon.com all have affiliate programs. Do you?

An affiliate is someone who will promote your products or services in return for a commission on any sales they refer to you. For digital products, the most common commission is 50% because of the high margins. For physical products, the commissions could range anywhere from 2% to 30%.

What commission should you offer your affiliates? It all depends on your margins and what will attract the most successful affiliates. Obviously, you should still be able to earn a profit after paying out your affiliate commissions. Make sure you do the math beforehand to ensure that you're not paying too high of a commission and end up losing money on the deal.

When an affiliate program is structured properly, you will earn more profits and so will your affiliates. That's a win-win.

~ ACTION STEP ~

If you don't have an affiliate program, consider starting one. Be generous with your affiliate commissions you offer (while remaining profitable) and provide useful information for your affiliates including swipe copy for emails, banner ads, sample Tweets and Facebook status updates and custom tracking links. The more training and tools you offer your affiliates, the more sales they will generate for your business.

There are many affiliate plugins for WordPress as well as more advanced affiliate management solutions depending on your needs.

8. Online Joint Venture Partners

A JOINT VENTURE (JV) is a business partnership with another business or individual. The sky is the limit when it comes to joint ventures. There truly are an infinite number of ways you can arrange a JV.

Most commonly, a joint venture online is where two business owners who sell complimentary or similar digital products agree to promote each other's products through each other's affiliate program. This way, both parties increase their sales as well as make a commission for promoting the complimentary product.

Other common ways to structure a JV include adding a bonus "free report" or free bonus to your current offering from your promotional partner. This adds more value to your product offering and allows your JV partner to grow their exposure when people read their free report after purchasing your product.

> **~ ACTION STEP ~**
>
> Research some of your "competitors" and turn them into joint venture partners! Collaborating with the competition could be a great way to increase your sales and profits. Most entrepreneurs are afraid to talk to the competition, but I've found that it's often the fastest way to earning more profits, and it's incredibly rewarding.
>
> You can also contact companies that sell related products and approach them about joint venture opportunities. For example, if you sell a nutritional supplement, you could JV with a health coach. You could promote their service, and they could promote your product, for example. Always be looking for new joint venture partners.

9. Create a Podcast or Web TV Show

HAVING A SHOW is an extremely powerful way to take advantage of new media to grow your business and reach a broader audience.

A podcast is like a radio show that people listen to online. Many podcast listeners download shows on their iPods or iPhones and listen while they commute, work out or do busy work. Podcasts can be either audio online or video and audio. I recommend creating an audio-only podcast and publishing it on iTunes.

If you create video, I would recommend uploading your videos to YouTube.

For my Publishing Profits Podcast show[4], I interview bestselling authors, publishers, marketers, and PR experts on what it takes to succeed today as an author. I record all the interviews in video format using Google Hangouts. Then, we post the video interviews on YouTube, and we convert the video file to an mp3 audio file and publish only the audio on iTunes (you can subscribe to the show on iTunes[5]).

That way, I get exposure from the interviews in video format on the massive YouTube network as well as getting tons of exposure in audio format on iTunes. One interview is published to multiple platforms, giving me more exposure for the same amount of work.

If you're already recording videos or audio files and you don't have a podcast show, you're missing out on a lot of free traffic and exposure. You can start a podcast for free at www.podomatic.com

If you're looking for a higher-end solution, you can host your own podcast on your blog like I do at Publishing Profits Podcast. I then pay about $15 a month for audio hosting with www.Libsyn.com, and I use the Blubrry Powerpress Podcasting plugin for WordPress[6], which is free, to publish the show on iTunes.

---

[4] www.publishingprofitspodcast.com
[5] https://itunes.apple.com/us/podcast/publishing-profits-podcast/id788984301
[6] https://WordPress.org/plugins/powerpress

> **~ ACTION STEP ~**
>
> Start your own podcast show!
>
> You can get started for free at:
> **www.podomatic.com**
>
> or create a Podcast within your own blog using WordPress.
>
> For audio recordings, you can use Audacity to record and edit audio for free.
>
> For Video recordings, you can use Camtasia or Skype Telecorder for PC, as well as Google Hangouts which is free.
>
> If you have a Mac you can use Screenflow, Skype Recorder or Google Hangouts.

10. Blogging

ONE OF THE things I'm best known for in the online marketing world is blogging. I took a brand new blog from 0 to over 100,000 page views a month in just 9 months without spending a dime on advertising, SEO or paid traffic!

But even if you're not a blogging expert you can still use this incredible marketing strategy.

Anyone can create a blog for free and be up and running in 30 minutes. The problem with most small business owners is that they don't understand how to start a blog or create their own websites so they're stuck at the mercy of web designers who overcharge you. I've even seen small businesses spend $50,000 on a cheap website that I could have built in 8 hours with less than $200!

I've created a tutorial video that you can use to build your own self-hosted WordPress blog right away and start getting tons of free traffic as well. You can watch the trainings for free at:

www.BlogBusinessSchool.com

11. Guest Blogging

As long as you have a website or something you're selling online, guest blogging can be an incredibly powerful marketing strategy. The best thing is that it's 100% free!

Searching for the Right Blogs

To start with guest blogging, you want to search for other blogs in your niche OR in niches that are similar or compatible with yours so that you can build a relationship with them and share your info with their audience.

For example, if you have a blog about dog training, you could search for blogs about dogs, or blogs about dog training, or blogs about cats and cat training (you could write an article for them about dogs vs. cats - the never-ending debate!).

The key here is to think of AS MANY different types of niches that you could fit into and add value to, and that would add value to you as well.

Just remember to be open-minded - maybe horse training blogs would like you to write an article for them about the top 5 things you learned as a dog trainer and how that could be applied to horses. Be creative and you will find many more opportunities for collaboration, guest blogging and building links to your site.

Once you've picked your search term, let's say it's "dog training" for now, you're going to add blog to the end of that term. So you would go to Google.com, type in "dog training blog" and hit search!

Click and Analyze

At first, this step will take you a bit of time because you're just starting to learn how blogs work and how to navigate other peoples' sites.

Here are some general tips to make figuring out which sites to contact and which sites to ignore a whole lot easier:

First, if it's a news site, throw it out. For example, if you see well.blogs.newyorktimes.com in the search results, just skip past it - because I don't think the New York Times is going to accept your guest post... yet!

Second, if it's a duplicate site, only click one of them. Sometimes, Google will give you the same domain name several times in a search - so just click one of them and skip the extras. For example, you may see the following sites in the search results:

well.blogs.nytimes.com

business.blogs.nytimes.com

science.blogs.nytimes.com

If you see search results with several links from one domain there's no reason to click all of those links from the same website so just click one of them and move down the list until you find a link to a new domain.

Third, ignore spam blogs and low quality sites!

Here's a good example:

This site has a Google PageRank 2 - MUST BE A GREAT SITE TO GET A LINK FROM, RIGHT?

No way! It's Alexa rank is 15041954 - That means there are more than 15 million sites getting more traffic than that site - meaning it's essentially a garbage site that Google gives no traffic - and neither should you!

Do NOT solicit sites like this for links - even if you got a link from that site, it would do you more harm than good because it's quite likely Google has penalized that site for being spam, selling links, duplicate content or some other blackhat tricks.

If the Alexa Rank alone wasn't enough to let you know that site was not worth contacting just look at the home page! It says it's a weight loss blog and the home page article is just a spam advertisement for a "Coverking Stormproof Car" filled with affiliate links and ads!

If you see a site like this, close it out immediately and move on! (Also, if you get contacted by someone offering to sell or trade links from a site like that just ignore them!)

Don't do business with spammers - it will do more harm than good and could destroy your precious reputation with Google, especially early on!

What You're Looking For in a Good Blog

You're basically looking for quality sites with unique content that get traffic and are recognized by Google as being a legitimate, authoritative site.

Here are my general rules:

PageRank

The PageRank should be 1 or higher. When you're starting out, it's fine to guest post on lots of PR 1 or PR2 websites. As your blog grows in traffic, you may not have time to write for such sites and would want to write for PR 3 or higher sites (but it may take you a few months get to that point so be patient!)

Note: What Is Google PageRank?

Google PageRank is an indicator from 0 to 10 that tells you how much Google values a website in terms of its "authority." A site with a PageRank 0 has basically no authority (either because it's brand new or because it has no quality incoming links).

A site with a PageRank 10 has extremely high quality – and there are very few of them. Google and Twitter have PageRank 10. Facebook has a PageRank 9.

Contrary to what many SEO gurus will tell you, PageRank CANNOT tell you whether or not a site is worth getting a link from. Google now uses PageRank to "fool" SEO experts into thinking Google actually uses PageRank to determine search engine results – they don't!

For example, the spam site I showed you before with a PageRank 2 would NOT be worth getting a link from. In fact, if you had hundreds of links from sites like that, Google might even penalize your site.

This is why I only use PageRank as a general guide to whether or not a site is worth getting a link from – and I use other factors like the Alexa Rank and the site's own design and content to guide me.

Alexa Rank

When you first start out, any site with an Alexa Rank of 1,000,000 or lower should be just fine for guest posting. Basically, if a site is in the top 1 million sites, it's probably a decent site (just make sure the site LOOKS like a legitimate website too and is not really a spam site like the example above).

Note: What Is Alexa Rank?

Alexa is an independent website that monitors all the sites on the internet and ranks them in terms of their monthly, weekly and daily traffic and page views.

The Alexa Rank starts at 1 for the website with the most traffic in the world (currently Google) and counts up from there. Therefore, the lower your Alexa Rank, the better!

I use the Alexa Rank in conjunction with Google PageRank to make sure a site is legitimate and worthy of guest posting. For example, if a site has a Google PageRank 5 (A very nice, high PageRank) and an Alexa Rank of 12,231,221 (A very poor Alexa Rank), then I know something is amiss – it doesn't add up.

I would never solicit a link from a site like that because they are obviously using some kind of blackhat SEO techniques or they have been penalized by Google – either way, I want nothing to do with a site like that. And neither should you!

Site Layout and Content

The site needs to look human. If the only thing you see above the fold is Adsense ads in the header and sidebar, then it's probably a spam site. If it looks like a cookie-cutter website with no human elements to it, it's probably just junk.

If the site's domain is something like weightlossdieting.com but you actually look at the site and all the articles are about electronics, then it's probably a spam site. You want to make sure the site is "congruent" and that it actually looks like a legitimate website with useful information and that it's actively being managed by a real person.

Remember, you're looking for a site that looks like a **real person** actually manages it.

The Alexa Rank, Google PageRank and site design/content need to all be telling the same story – that this is a legitimate website with helpful information that gets a good amount of visitors on a daily basis. Otherwise, it's not worth getting a link from. Period.

Questionable Content

It pretty much goes without saying that you should avoid any sites that contain pornography, hate speech, illegal activities or anything that might shine a poor light on you and your business. Don't get caught up in trying to get links and forget that it's about quality first and quantity second!

Getting links from questionable sites will only hurt your traffic not help it.

Remember this before you ever hire someone else to build links to your website! Make sure you are reviewing the work they're doing and that they're not just sending spam links to your website. Many so-called SEO experts can do more harm than good when it comes to getting traffic to your site.

Contacting Bloggers

If the site looks like a real quality site, it's time to contact them!

Now you would be surprised but you will find many bloggers who have no way to contact them through their blog - they haven't listed their email address anywhere, there's no web form for contacting them, there's no "Contact Page," etc...

It's almost as if they don't want anyone to contact them!

These bloggers I just ignore - because if you can't find a way to contact them, chances are they aren't serious enough about blogging to waste your time trying to get in touch with them.

Most often, sites like this are free blogs hosted on Blogger or WordPress (the URL ends with a blogger or WordPress such as example.blogger.com or example.WordPress.com)

There are 3 main ways a blogger will post their contact information:

#1. Contact

They will have a web page called Contact or Contact Us - just use your keyboard to search for "contact."

NEAT TRICK:
Finding Text On A Web Page

On a PC you hit CTRL + F and type in the word you're searching for.

On a Mac, hit the Apple Command Button + F and type what you're searching for.

Either way, your computer will automatically find the letters or words you typed into the search box if they exist on the page.

If you don't see a contact page or form, then try to find the...

#2. About/About Me Page

Many times bloggers will have all their contact info in the About/About Me/About Us page of their site.

Just use that nifty search trick I taught you before and type in "about". If you don't see that, then try to find their contact info in the...

#3. Sidebar

Sometimes a blogger will list their contact info in the sidebar - so just look for it there if you can't find it elsewhere.

If that doesn't work, your last hope is...

#4. SOCIAL MEDIA

Some bloggers, either because they're tired of being spammed or they just don't know better, will only have their contact info for Twitter, a Facebook Fan Page or other social media accounts.

You can send them a tweet or message on the social network and see if they respond!

If that doesn't work then it's time to…

#5. MOVE ON

If steps 1-4 don't work, then just move on!

There are plenty of other high quality bloggers who actually care enough about their blog readers to provide contact info - these are the bloggers you want to work with!

Following Through

When a blog owner responds to your message, follow through!

If they ask you to write an article, write it promptly and send it to them and make sure it meets their guidelines and specifications. Make sure it's a HELPFUL article and not just promoting your blog - it should add real value to anyone who reads it.

You can do all the promotion you want of your own blog and your work in your author bio beneath the guest post.

See Guest Posting In Action

You can see one of my guest posts in action to get a feel for what they look like at the link in the footnotes[7].

In this post, my author bio appears before the article begins (although most bloggers put the author bio underneath it).

There's another example guest post[8] where my author bio appears below the post in a nice Author Box.

---

[7] http://ediblegoddess.com/2012/05/growing-your-own-fresh-produce-got-easier/
[8] http://socialmarketingwriting.com/5-reasons-guest-blogging-is-the-best-traffic-generator/

Sample Email To Blogger:

If you're not sure what to write to a blogger for a first-time contact, try something similar to this:

> Hi [Name],
>
> I love your blog! It's always inspiring to see others like you who are sharing the message of [Your Niche] in an easy to understand and exciting way.
>
> I'd love to see if there's some way we could collaborate with our sites through guest blogging, social media, or something else. I blog about [Your Niche] too. Check it out and let me know if you think it's a good fit. [Link To Your Site]
>
> [Salutation],
>
> [Your Name]

I always like to keep my emails short, sweet and to the point and customize them to the blogger I'm contacting. For example, if I notice an article on their site about their two adorable poodles, I might say "I love poodles too!" or something similar to let them know you actually read their blog.

What Not To Do

Here's an actual email sent to me by some spammer. Don't write like this!

Honestly, if you can't even write an email with good grammar and spelling how could you possibly write a good guest post for someone?

Horribly Written Email Which You Should Never Emulate

> "Hi,
>
> I saw your blog it is interesting, i want to introduce myself as a guest blogger. I have some interesting topics and contents are written by me after a short research..
>
> If you are interested let me know...Looking forward to write useful contents for your blog..
>
> Regards,
>
> John"

Thanks John! I'll be sure to let you know when I need horribly written articles for my blog.

Continue The Relationship With The Blogger

After you write a guest post for their site, maybe ask if they'd like to write a post for your site? Offer to help them in return.

Another great thing you should do when you guest post is to share the article you wrote in all of your social media channels – it helps promote their blog and it helps you too by showing your fans and followers that you're a credible authority, worthy of your articles being posted on other sites and blogs.

Always be creative and open to more ways to collaborate with other bloggers and website owners – we all win together if we help each other.

Don't just be a taker – be a giver too! Givers truly gain in the world of blogging.

12. Ebook Publishing and Marketing

A BOOK IS an incredibly powerful tool for any business! Don't believe me?

Well what business are you in? Write it down on a piece of paper like this:

> "I am in the business of helping [describe the kind of customers you help]
> with [describe the problem your customers have]
> by [describe your solution to their problem]."

For example, if you sell jewelry, you might answer something like this:

> "I am in the business of helping fashion-savvy women age 25-45 look more beautiful and feel better about themselves by selling high quality, chic jewelry."

Ok great! Well why not write a book for women age 25-45 teaching them how to pick out the right jewelry that complements their style?

You could write a short eBook called *5 Pieces Of Jewelry Every Woman Must Own* and then in the book provide useful, helpful and interesting information about jewelry that will educate your prospects and customers about how to be better consumers. At the end of the book you can list information in regards to your website, contact information and even a special offer or coupon for your jewelry!

If you only sold 100 books a month that's over 1200 new prospects a year for your business! But these aren't just any old prospects. These are RED HOT prospects who already KNOW your brand, TRUST your brand, have a COUPON for your brand and obviously love jewelry enough to pay for and read a book about it.

Not sure how to publish an eBook? The easiest thing to do is just write it in a word document, hire someone for $100 or so to edit and format it for Amazon Kindle and post it on Amazon.com (the whole process takes less than 15 minutes to post it on Amazon). You can watch my free video trainings on how to write, publish and market your eBooks at:

www.EbookPublishingSchool.com

If you just want more prospects for your business you can give the book away for free or you can charge for it. It's up to you whether you want to earn royalties and new prospects or just maximize the number of prospects by giving away the book.

By the way, you're not limited to just one book – you can write as many as you like!

And if you're not into writing, you can hire a ghostwriter to write the book for you for a few hundred dollars for a short eBook. Just post a classified Ad for free on Craigslist.com in the San Francisco Writing Gigs section and you'll get dozens of responses!

~ ACTION STEP ~

Decide if you would like to write your eBook yourself or hire someone to do it. If you're planning on doing it yourself, start now! Open a new document and start typing. Just a few words will do to get the project started.

If you're planning on hiring a writer, then post a listing on Craigslist now and you'll soon have several applicants who you can interview and find the best ghostwriter for your needs.

13. Pay-Per-Click Ads

PAY-PER-CLICK (PPC) ads are online ads that run on websites such as Facebook, Google and just about any other site online. When someone clicks on your advertisement, you pay per click. The cost could range anywhere from 1 cent to $20 a click depending on which advertising network you use.

I highly recommend Facebook Ads first and foremost for any new advertisers. Their ad program is incredibly affordable and very easy to use for beginners.

I would recommend avoiding Google AdWords for beginner – it's highly competitive and it takes either an expert or someone who's willing to dedicate hundreds of hours and a lot of study to turn it into a profitable campaign.

With Facebook though, you can start a campaign for as little as $1 a day and start seeing instant results.

You can even get coupons for $50, $75 or even $100 in free ad credits.

~ ACTION STEP ~

Check out:

www.Facebook.com/ads

today and get started.

14. Squidoo

SQUIDOO IS A great website for posting articles, videos and useful content. You can earn money from the advertising on your squidoo pages as well as sales from your page as well as sales on your own website by attracting leads from Squidoo.

On Squidoo, you can create a lens. A lens is like an article or web page that you create on Squidoo and customize it any way you want with videos, pictures and all kinds of cool widgets.

Similar to the eBook strategy mentioned before, you can just write an informative article that your target customers would appreciate and find valuable and link to your website for customers who would like to purchase more.

If you have pictures of your products, post those on your lens and turn it into a new shopping page outside of your own website!

> ### ~ ACTION STEP ~
> Just go to:
> **www.squidoo.com**
> sign up for a new account and create a lens.

15. Video Marketing

VIDEO MARKETING IS hot, hot, hot right now!

More people go online to watch video than any other form of media – which means if you're not using online video, you're missing out on over 50% of your potential customers!

I know we've already talked about YouTube but that's just one way to use video for your business. Online marketers are now finding that video sales pages convert up to 127% MORE than sales pages without video!

This means that simply by recording a simple sales video, you can dramatically increase your online sales!

Even Zappos is now using online video on their product sales pages to describe their shoes, clothing and products to potential customers. Think about it – if someone's going to take the effort to go all the way to your product sales page, shouldn't you give them ALL the information they need to make a good buying decision?

Just a simple video showing the customer your product could clinch that sale, dramatically improving your online conversions and profits.

What have you got to lose? Create a 1-2 minute sales video for your online products and test it out!

~ ACTION STEP ~

Record a short video that features your product or service and add it to your sales page!

16. Search Engine Optimization

SEARCH ENGINE OPTIMIZATION (SEO) is a set of principles, ideas and techniques for improving your website's rankings in search engines.

But you don't need to be an SEO guru to do SEO! In fact, I recommend not listening to SEO gurus – because 90% of them are full of crap!

They'll tell you to get automated software to spam comments on thousands of blogs or they'll sell you a package of 1,000 web 2.0 backlinks – but what's the point? Do you honestly think that you can get 1,000 links for a few hundred dollars (or $5 on Fiverr.com) and that those links will actually help you get more sales? No way!

16. SEARCH ENGINE OPTIMIZATION 51

Google and the other search engines are way too smart to fall for that these days. If anything, buying links like that will get your website penalized by Google or even de-indexed if you do it over and over.

The key to effective online SEO is to write for people not search engines. If you post great, engaging, useful content on your blog or website, people will share it naturally. And it's that sharing that creates viral traffic, high quality backlinks to your site and in the end better search engine rankings.

So don't worry about using the perfect SEO keywords – worry about the ONLY THING THAT MATTERS IN BUSINESS – helping your customers!

If you post great content on your website that honestly helps your customers solve their problems, you will get more search engine traffic – guaranteed.

~ ACTION STEP ~

Think about your current SEO strategy.
Do you even have one?
Think about how you can create amazing online content that people will naturally want to share.
What do your customers really need or want?
What information would they love to see?

17. Offer A Free Report

THIS STRATEGY IS very similar to the eBook strategy except instead of selling an eBook, you're giving away a free report in return for capturing your prospect's email address so that you can continue to market to them via email.

The report could be an eBook, a video training course, a series of interviews, whatever you want! The key is that your free offer should be helpful to your customers, desirable to your customers and easy to consume.

First, you want to offer something helpful to your customers. It should solve a problem they have – preferably a big problem!

For example, if you have a dog training business, offer a free training video on how to potty train a dog or how to get your dog to stop barking. These are some pretty big problems for dog owners, right? If you can solve one of those problems with a simple video or report, those prospects will buy more training from you and not from your competitors!

Next, the offer should be desirable. Even though a video on how to potty train your dog would be helpful, it might not be desirable to every potential customer of yours. Maybe most of your visitors already have a dog that's potty trained. In that case, you should come up with a free offer that's desirable to a broader segment of your customer base to increase your opt ins and leads.

Lastly, your report should be easy to consume. A 5-minute video on potty training a dog is easy to consume. A 4-hour lecture on the theory of classical conditioning vs. modern dog training philosophy is hard to consume!

Don't give your customers too much – make it EASY for them to use the information you've given them. Otherwise, you're just going to overwhelm them, they won't use the information and they'll forget all about you.

Just give them a small taste of what you can do and make it easy for them – then ask them to come back and buy for even more!

> **~ ACTION STEP ~**
>
> If you're writing an eBook like we mentioned before you can use that as your free report! Otherwise, come up with some other gifts you can offer – a video training, special interview or something else.

18. Article Writing

WRITING ARTICLES IS a powerful way to connect with your prospects online.

You can write articles on your niche or areas of expertise and publish them on sites like **http://Ezinearticles.com** and **http://Goarticles.com**

You can even outsource article writing by hiring a writer using Craigslist.

> **~ ACTION STEP ~**
> Write two articles or hire a writer to do so and post one to EzineArticles and the other to GoArticles.

19. Create a Song

THIS MARKETING STRATEGY is almost never used which is one of the reasons why it's so powerful.

First of all, I'm not asking you to become a professional musician. All you have to do is hire a college student in music school or a freelancer to create a song for you on a budget. You can probably get it done for less than $1,000 easily. Today with computer software like Garageband, any musical hobbyist can create professional music very easily.

So what's the point of your song? The point is to connect with your customers – like all good marketing!

For example, Mountain Dew created a song about Mountain Dew in the form of an Irish drinking song[9].

---

[9] http://bit.ly/UembMy

It's hilarious, entertaining and it's been heard by millions of people all over the world.

By the way, that's just one version of the song above. It's been re-done and re-mixed many times over. They key with this strategy is to create an entertaining, fun and/or funny song that people will naturally share with their friends. It's viral marketing at its best!

~ ACTION STEP ~

Find someone to create a song for your business! You can again use Craigslist to find someone in the gigs section or call your local college and tell them you'd like to hire a music student for a special project.

20. Create Something Outrageous

ANYTIME YOU CAN create something online that's outrageous, wild, hilarious or ridiculous, people are likely to talk about it, link to it and share it – meaning more traffic, links and potential customers for you.

For example, CollegeHumor created a video of Barack Obama and Mitt Romney as if they were a fighters in a video game[10].

Something like this might seem out of place for your business but think again – what can you create that's hilarious, wild or outrageous that connects with your brand? Maybe you could create a spoof of the hit show "The Office" at your own office.

---

[10] http://huff.to/RpTZYT

20. CREATE SOMETHING OUTRAGEOUS

All I know is that doing something outrageous is a great way to get people talking about your business – and if people aren't talking about your business you'll soon be out of business!

> **~ ACTION STEP ~**
>
> Brainstorm some outrageous marketing products, videos or ideas you can create to reach a bigger audience.

21. Create a Membership Site or Program

CREATE A MEMBERSHIP site for your customers!

A membership program is a program your customers can subscribe to and pay a monthly fee to belong to. You might be thinking, "Well creating a new product isn't really marketing!" But it is!

It's the best kind of marketing – marketing to your existing customers. Any successful business owner knows it's far easier to sell more product to their existing customers than to find new customers and sell to them.

You wouldn't believe the kind of membership programs people have come up with!

There's the "Boxer of the Month club" where you can pay $15-$20 a month and receive a new pair of boxers every month.

There's even a "Candy of the Month Club" for $25 a month where you can get a new shipment of candy sent to your house every month.

Then there are digital membership programs where someone pays to become a member of a website and doesn't receive any physical product.

Netflix is one of the biggest examples with over 30 million active subscribers. There are dieting membership sites, how to make money online membership sites and pretty much anything else you can think of!

The great thing about owning a membership program is that it dramatically increases your business's revenue and stabilizes your cash flow, especially for seasonal businesses like retail.

How does offering a membership program dramatically increase your revenue?

Think about it – would a customer be more likely to pay $1000 upfront for a large purchase of (name your products) or would they be more likely to pay $100 a month for a year, two years or even longer?

You can increase the lifetime value of your customers by offering membership programs in conjunction with your current product offerings.

~ ACTION STEP ~

Brainstorm some ideas for a possible membership program.

Do you want to offer a digital membership site, create a membership program offering some of your product on a monthly basis or just create a special VIP program for your customers who want priority service?

After you're done brainstorming, pick the membership program you think will be most successful and start on it.

I didn't say pick the easiest one to do – pick the one you think will provide the best level of service to your customers!

22. Blogger Product Reviews

DO YOU THINK your business would grow if you had hundreds of bloggers spreading your message for you?

Then why don't you start building relationships with bloggers so they can do all the hard marketing work for you?

Here's how...

There's a website called Tomoson[11]. It's free to sign up both for bloggers or businesses. The site connects bloggers and businesses in order to provide product reviews and giveaways.

---

[11] www.tomoson.com/

Basically, you can create a posting on the site which other bloggers will see offering one of your products for free as a review product. Then, the blogger will try your product and write a review and post it on the blog for their audience to see.

You can choose which bloggers to work with and even screen bloggers by criteria like the Alexa Rank or PageRank of their blog or the size of their social media following.

~ ACTION STEP ~

Create an account at:

www.Tomoson.com

and create a free posting.

If you want to do even more, research bloggers in your niche or industry and contact them to see if they're open to doing a product review.

23. Coupon Sites

COUPON SITES LIKE Groupon are also a mixture between the online and offline world – but at the end of the day the point is to create a new customer.

Ever since Groupon came out in 2009, the media has been talking about how good online coupons are for driving sales. The truth is many small business owners have lost a lot of money using Groupon. This is because they made a fatal mistake!

These businesses were often small local businesses like a coffee shop or bakery that would offer a coupon for a free coffee or free muffin or something like that.

That's all fine and good but if you're going to offer a free coupon for a physical product like a muffin, you have to do some math before you start.

First of all, how much revenue and profit does your store make in one day? If you're going to offer a free product for one day only, you better know how much you earn on a regular day without a promotion.

Next, you've got to calculate how many shifts you will have to add to handle all the increased traffic – as well as the cost of delivering the product itself.

Let's say for example, on a normal day you help 200 customers and make $1,000 profit. So you run a 1-day coupon on Groupon for a free muffin with no restrictions.

Then 1,000 people come in asking for a free muffin. How much is that going to cost you to deliver the muffins? How long will the lines be? How many of your regular customers will be upset because there's a line of 50 people all trying to get a free muffin and your loyal customer just wants the regular?

The key with any promotion like this is that you don't want to piss off the customers you already have. It's all fine and good to get new customers but it's very important to keep your existing customers happy!

So how can you do it?

First of all, provide a limit to every offer. If you normally help 200 customers a day and you know that your peak capacity is 400 customers a day then only offer a maximum of 200 free muffins. It sounds so simple – but you wouldn't believe how many business owners fail to do that!

ALWAYS include a limiter when you're offering free product.

As long as you plan ahead, a coupon promotion can be a great way to attract new customers. Just make sure it's a special promotion and not something you do every week – because then you'll just attract a bunch of customers who only want free stuff.

Finally, consider offering your own promotions instead of using a company like Groupon that takes up to 50% or your earnings. You can use Facebook Offers to let people know about a coupon or promotion, for example, and reach thousands of potential customers for just a few dollars – just remember to include a limiter!

> ### ~ ACTION STEP ~
> Would a coupon or special promotion be a good fit for your business?
>
> If so then consider using Facebook Offers and test out your new promotion.

24. MEETUP.COM

MEETUP.COM is the perfect blend between online and offline marketing! It's a fantastic way to connect with people locally both online and offline.

"My most successful offline marketing strategy is leveraging MeetUp.com to find local groups, but I do it with a methodical twist that yields great, consistent results.

Here's my 5 step approach:

Step 1

I search MeetUp.com for appropriate groups, but I'm very selective. It's important to me to spend my time wisely, therefore I only attend functions where my target demographic is well represented. I also seek out groups that are educational based, bringing in regular speakers to help increase the groups knowledge base.

Step 2

I always contact the group facilitator via email in advance to create initial rapport. By connecting via email, they can see my signature, visit my website and start to have an idea of who I am. It may sound basic, but most people don't do this. It's a 5-minute task that truly adds impact to the initial impression.

Step 3

Once at the function, I quickly establish myself as an expert in my niche by being generous with information wherever I can contribute value. I love helping other business owners succeed, and this natural approach showcases my expertise to the group facilitator while quickly connecting me with others in the group.

Step 4

I go to the ladies room and write a quick thank you card to the facilitator. If I've determined this is a group I resonate with and want to regularly participate in, then my thank you includes:

- My business card
- A note complimenting something specific from this event, and expressing how much I look forward to the next one
- A P.S. extending an offer to help in any way

Step 5

I follow up with a quick video message 1 - 2 days after the event and include an offer to donate a business-related raffle prize or to speak at a future meeting.

This approach has led to numerous opportunities including: dozens of new clients, additional speaking opportunities with other groups, radio interviews and more.

In a few months I'll be relocating from Atlanta to Denver. I have no professional ties in Denver, but with this approach, I also have no worries about getting reestablished!"

Laura Waage,
LauraWaage.com

~ ACTION STEP ~

Sign up at MeetUp.com and find local groups in your area where you can network and meet potential customers and business partners.

Part 2

Offline Marketing

Now we're going to cover more traditional offline marketing strategies. Some of these are free but many will require a small investment upfront in your business.

25. Business Cards

BUSINESS CARDS SAY a lot about you. Take out your business card right now and look at it – what does it say about you and your business? Often your business card will be the second impression someone gets of your business.

First they meet you. If they like you, good. That's a plus. Second, they see your card. If they like it, great! They'll now be more comfortable with your business. But if your card turns them off it could ruin the deal!

So what does your business card say about you?

Is it clean?

Your business cards should always be clean and look immaculate. If they're dirty, torn, bent or look worn just throw them out!

Does it look professional?

25. BUSINESS CARDS

It should be designed either by a professional or with a professional looking template. Don't try to make your own business card using your Printer and cut them out by hand! I've actually been handed a "business card" like that before. This shows a huge lack of professionalism and reflects poorly on you and your business. It basically says either " don't care about doing things professionally" or "I'm too poor to buy quality business cards" – either way it's not good.

Is it what you want to represent your brand?

Does your card reflect your company's brand or does it say "Printed by vistaprint.com" on the back?

Do you think the CEO of Vistaprint would ever hand someone a business card that advertises YOUR business? Of course not! So why should you advertise his business?

The same holds true for email addresses. If your business card says Tom@yahoo.com people think you're a yahoo! Professional business owners have an email that's branded with your own domain. For example, yourname@yourwebsite.com.

CASE STUDY

"You can promote yourself and your business in an instant. However trite it sounds, you never get a second chance to make a first impression

For instance, business cards are only as effective as far as recipient takes them. I work for a company that provides consulting and testing on technology for people with disabilities. Many people we work either with or for are blind or have low vision. Sometimes, handing them a business card is akin to giving a person a blank sheet of paper.

In order to make sure our business cards are in the best format for everyone, we made sure we took some extra steps. First, we emboss all of our cards in Braille with our website and telephone number. On the back of our card, we provide our contact information in larger font for those with low vision. In addition, we've made sure that our cards have good color contrast and clear font.

I want my marketing to reach everyone, and my efforts have ensured that I can."

Dana Marlowe,
AccessibilityPartners.com

25. BUSINESS CARDS

> **~ ACTION STEP ~**
>
> Look at your business card. Does it reflect your brand and look professional? If not, hire someone to design a new card for you!
>
> If you need a new domain for your email, you can use GoDaddy[12] to purchase a new domain for about $10 and they'll set up a custom email address for you.
>
> If you have your own domain already, just call your domain name registrar and they'll set you up with a custom email address.

---

[12] http://www.jdoqocy.com/click-5271137-10386906

26. Write For Newspapers and Publications

NEWSPAPERS, MAGAZINES, TRADE journals and other publications are always looking for great articles, advice and useful information to publish. Why not help by providing them with your great article so you can reach more people?

All these publications are happy to include your name, company name and contact information which is how your articles will generate leads and new business for you.

26. WRITE FOR NEWSPAPERS & PUBLICATIONS

> **~ ACTION STEP ~**
>
> Research your local newspaper and any industry magazines or publications you admire.
>
> Contact them about becoming a contributor and ask how you can help.

27. Volunteer

COMMUNITY SERVICE HAS long been intertwined with business and every single successful business person I know is involved in some kind of community service project.

If you volunteer to help or sit on a non-profit board, you will find other like-minded business professionals with whom you can network, build relationships and do future deals with.

~ ACTION STEP ~

What causes or organizations are you passionate about?

Don't just join an organization to meet people – join because you care and really want to contribute. You'll naturally meet the right people if you approach it with the right attitude.

Contact the organization you most want to work with and see how you can get involved.

28. Join the SBA Small Business Mentoring Program

THE SMALL BUSINESS Administration (SBA) has a huge number of volunteers who help mentor small business owners. Often, these volunteers are retired entrepreneurs who just want to give back and help new business owners get on the right track.

You can get a meeting with these mentors for free. Just check out the SBA[13] and find a local branch, call them and set up a time to meet. Often, these mentors will not only provide you with advice on your business but they'll also refer you to potential customers, clients and business partners.

---

[13] www.sba.gov/

28. JOIN THE SMALL BUSINESS MENTORING PROGRAM

~ **ACTION STEP** ~
Contact your local SBA office
and get a meeting with a mentor.

29. Write A Book

ONCE YOU'RE AN author, you become an instant expert in your area (at least according to people's perception). This can dramatically increase your sales and opportunities.

Case Study

"One of my strategies is to carry three copies of my book *Speak Louder Than Words* whenever I attend a networking function or large event for business people. Having books in front of me has often led to conversations and questions. The presence of a book gives me so on-the-spot gravitas about being an expert in my area which is to help visionary entrepreneurs and business leaders with their message and then how to deliver it effectively kin front of groups

The reason I bring three is that it creates a different look than just one so it's a bit more eye-catching. Having multiple copies allows me to share the book with a leader who expresses particular interest. It's gotten me a chance to give it to speakers at events, and led to the book being excerpted in SmartCEO Magazine as well as my being used as an expert in an article on Entreprenuer.com

As a result of this strategy I frequently leave these meetings with an appointment for a consultation and it has led to several new private clients I might not otherwise have met -- and they initiated the conversations with me."

John Rasiej, Public Speaking Mentor,
speaklouderthanwordsbook.com

> ### ~ ACTION STEP ~
> Have you dreamed of writing a book? Does this marketing strategy resonate with you? If so, start! All it takes is a few words a day and you'll have a full book completed rapidly.
>
> For those of you who have trouble writing, you can simply have someone interview you and then have a ghostwriter turn your interview into the book!

30. Phone Calls

IT AMAZES ME how rarely businesses take advantage of the telephone these days. Everyone wants to use automated emails and phone answering programs instead of actually talking to a real human being over the phone.

Do I love automated marketing? You bet! But there's something powerful about talking face-to-face or on the phone that can never be emulated by an email or a recorded voice on answering machine.

Phone calls are especially effective when it comes to selling high ticket items and providing customer service when a customer has a problem. If you're just selling a $27 digital eBook, no big deal – you probably don't need phone support. You will lose sales from customers who would like to speak on the phone before purchasing but the amount may be insignificant for most online marketers.

But when it comes to selling higher-ticket items like a $1,000 coaching package or a $2,000 seminar, you're going to lose a massive amount of sales if you're not using phone calls as part of your marketing and closing strategy.

CUSTOMER SERVICE PHONE CALLS

Phone calls aren't just important for making sales – they're important for keeping your customers happy! If a customer has a problem, get on the phone and help them out! You can turn an unhappy customer into a lifelong customer with just a simple phone call – just by showing you care.

Caring is one of the things so blatantly missing from corporate business today. I ordered a plane ticket online from American Airlines the other day and there was a problem so I called their customer support. After waiting an hour, I did some research and found out American Airlines doesn't actually take phone calls. That's right – "we're not set up to make phone calls" said their "customer service" on Twitter!

How ridiculous is that? A multi-billion dollar Fortune 500 company that doesn't take phone calls. Absurd!

But this is exactly why making phone calls can set you apart from your competition – because most of your competition isn't doing it. And if they are, there's a lot of bad phone support staff out there – the kind that are rude, don't listen, talk too much and are generally unhelpful. Train your staff differently!

A Quick Fix

Want to fix a customer's complaint fast? Just have the CEO of your company call them. That's right, just have the CEO make a 2-minute phone call to the customer. If there was a problem, the CEO can apologize immediately and offer to solve the problem in a mutually beneficial way. If there's no problem, the CEO can just thank the customer for being a loyal customer. You wouldn't believe how many people your customers will share that story with!

"You wouldn't believe it, Jim! The CEO of So-and-So company called ME personally to thank me for being a customer. I've never gotten a call from a CEO before!"

Little things make a big difference when it comes to marketing.

~ ACTION STEP ~

If you don't have phone support for customer service, get it! You're missing out on sales otherwise.

If you already have phone support, check your quality control. How do you and your employees answer the phone? Do you allow your customer support staff to solve problems on their own or do they have to ask a manager and go up the chain of command to finally help the customer get what they want (and what they probably should have gotten in the first place).

Lastly, consider making phone calls to your current and past customers just to personally thank them for doing business with you.

31. Customer Marketing

SOMETIMES IT'S BEST to let your customers do the marketing for you!

But it's not always that easy – and often they won't do it without a little creativity and planning ahead of time on your part. One of the easiest and quickest ways to let your customers market for you is to use social media like Twitter and Facebook and ask your customers to share with their friends every time they order.

Case Study

"I find that the people who are really growing, are doing what I call "megaphone marketing". The whole strategy of megaphone marketing is about really growing through the people who like you, who respect you, and who have a vested interest in your success.

These people are willing to listen to you, willing to take your call, and these people are warm (meaning you have earned permission to send them personal, anticipated and relevant messages) and they love you. So if you hand them a megaphone and if all of them are talking about how great your organization, product or service is, suddenly the warm leads multiply. And warm is critical because cold doesn't work as well as it used to, but warm, the people who will give you permission to send them messages, go up.

Where does the megaphone live? The megaphone lives offline, on bumper stickers for people's car, business cards, coupons, at organized classes that teach people, and etc. One unique example of this are tourist rides in particular cities, where these old world war two boats drive through the city and then drive into the river as a boat. And what they do is give everyone on the boat a duck calling device.

Now, why would they do that? The answer is because tourist usually are walking around and while they're walking around, this boat full of happy tourist making duck sounds goes by. Someone then asks, "who was that?" And other ask someone who got off the boat, "what company was that?"

The megaphone was the duck device that the happy and enthusiastic tourist was eager to use. So what you have the opportunity to do now if you hurry, is go to those people who you have permission to talk to and hand them a megaphone, and say, 'here's a place you can do it offline.'"

Patrick McFadden, Blogger,
Marketer, & Teacher
mcfaddencoaching.com

~ ACTION STEP ~

Brainstorm some ways you can get your customers to share your message.

How can you empower them to do so?

Maybe you can offer a bundle package with a brander T-shirt or other merchandise for your customers to help them spread the message.

Maybe you need to calls to action to let your customers know to connect with your brand on Facebook and Twitter.

32. Hosting An Event

HOSTING AND CREATING events can be a powerful way to market to people in your community (or all over the world depending on the size of your event!)

You can host a conference, a public education lecture (or series of lectures), a party or anything you can imagine. Be creative and have fun with it!

If there's one thing that makes a good marketing event it's fun – because if it's not fun people won't share your message and they sure as heck won't show up at the next event.

You can create a fundraising event to raise money for a local charity. You can create a community party to celebrate a new milestone in your company or a product launch. You can host a conference for people in your industry to connect, learn and collaborate.

How Do Events Bring In Sales?

You can have booths at the event where employees or salespeople talk to prospects and make sales. You can speak in front of the whole group and tell them about your company and services. You can have your branding all over the event. You can get free press coverage thanks to the event. You can get interviewed in the media about the event. You can get sponsors for the event.

There are so many ways to monetize an event!

~ ACTION STEP ~
Plan an event!

Make it fun, educational, inspiring and uplifting. Make it something to talk about. And make sure it matches with your brand and your message!

33. Create A Branded Product

IF YOUR PRODUCT isn't unique or branded then it just becomes a commodity. Think of buying keys, for example. When's the last time you bought keys or had duplicate keys made? Do you even remember? Are keys a brand or a commodity? They're just a commodity!

But the only reason keys are a commodity is because no one has built a brand around them that you or I recognize. But you can build a brand around ANY product if you put your mind to it!

Case Study

"Our marketing approach is to invest in our brand. As locksmiths, we had to think outside the box on marketing and figure out a way to be present in the everyday lives of our customers.

Everyone interacts with locks and keys in a daily basis. Carrying keys are a fact of life and we wanted to be a part of this daily reality for our customers. We decided to mill our own key blanks with our logo and phone number and make our customers part of our marketing campaign simply by carrying their keys. Several people go to big box retailers for a duplicate key only because they aren't aware of their local locksmith. With our brand and number on each key, we have circumvented key cutting confusion.

In addition, we all interact with locks, when we open the door at the local ice cream parlor or visit a shopping center. Usually, the item that is at eye level is the face of the lock - right next to the door pull/handle. We carefully designed metallic stickers to fit in the front of the locks, again with our brand and phone number, and use the store fronts of our customers for awareness. This has been very successful for us.

We are a 95 year old, 4th generation family business, and have built a reputation based on solid customer service and quality. Our last name is synonymous with locks, but with the constant growth of our community, we decided to be proactive and engage our community with these simple, yet effective, marketing tactics. Investing in your brand is the best decision a small business can make, in conjunction with, superior customer service and fostering an internal culture of excellence."

David E. Saucedo II,
saucedocompany.com

When's the last time you saw a key like that with a brand and phone number on it? That's great marketing and branding!

Remember, always, that your product is a huge part of your brand. So if you deliver a physical product, don't commoditize it! Brand your product if you want to grow your brand!

~ ACTION STEP ~

Look at the product or service you're delivering right now. Be totally honest with yourself – is it a commodity or is it a brand?

What makes it unique and different from what any other company anywhere in the world is offering?

The truth is, there's NOTHING different between Saucedo's keys and any other keys you'll find out there – but they branded their keys. Their keys are out there marketing for them 24/7. Every time a customer pulls out their keys, they see the Saucedo brand and phone number. How many sales do you think that has led to?

How could you possibly hope to compete in a commodity market like that WITHOUT branding your product?

If your product isn't branded right now come up with some ideas on paper of ways you can brand it!

If you offer a service, come up with ways you can brand your service! For example, you can send thank you letters to new customers, offer a bonus, gifts or an extra service add-on for free. Whatever you do just do something different than what everyone else is doing!

34. Public Speaking

FOR MANY PROFESSIONALS and small business owners, public speaking can be the most effective form of marketing on the planet.

Case Study

"We recently launched the first ever Non-Profit Medical Science Liaison Society and utilized public speaking opportunities to help successfully launch the society. It took 2.5 years to create this and over the last year we have implemented an offline strategy that has consisted of attending and speaking at numerous international conferences and meetings to build awareness and membership. I have spoken at a number already and scheduled at a number more in the next several months.

We also created a publication marketing plan that consists of getting both articles in industry related blogs and industry journals published. We have a number of them scheduled for the next several months. I also recently was a guest on a radio program for the pharmaceutical industry. Lastly I am also authoring a book on the MSL role that is expected to be published next spring that will further highlight the society that has received some publicity.

All of this marketing resulted in us having a very successful first live event about 2 weeks ago where we had over 600 people around the world register for the event."

Dr. Samuel Dyer,
Chairman of the Board,
Medical Science Liaison Society, themsls.org

~ ACTION STEP ~

If you like speaking, start letting people know that you're available for public lectures. If you offer to do a free lecture you'll find a lot of takers!

If you don't like speaking in public, join Toastmasters and start practicing. Although public speaking is the #1 fear even above death it's really not all that bad – in fact it's fun. And it's great marketing!

How To Book Speaking Gigs

"I learned early on that getting in front of one client at a time would not build the business fast enough. It was imperative that I get in front of a lot of people quickly, but I had little money to spend on marketing.

I needed to think outside the box and find low cost ways to get the public to know me and what I can do for them. I became very good at marketing and media relations, which enabled me to build the business quickly.

One strategy I implemented was to go to all the local libraries and review their card file for local clubs and organizations that might have the need for a speaker at their meetings. I then set up a campaign where twice a year I sent everyone on my list a letter offering to be a speaker as a free public service for their meeting or conference. I included my bio and a one page overview with bullet points outlining topics I was qualified to speak about that would be appropriate specifically for their members.

After four years, I found myself either on the radio, television, or in print at least monthly for the next twenty-five years. And the only cost to me was the mailing campaign I sent out twice a year."

Nancy D. Butler, CFP(r), CDFA(tm), CLTC, aboveallelse.org

35. Turning Cold Calls Into Warm Calls

IS THERE A certain big client you would love to have as a customer? Sometimes if you can't reach them by making a cold call (or you don't want to), it can be a lot easier to get your foot in the door by turning it into a warm call.

You can do this by just going to the business and building a relationship with someone there – maybe a salesperson or secretary.

Once you have a relationship with someone in the company, they can introduce you to the decision maker and you can get to business.

Case Study

"One of my favorite offline marketing strategies is to go shopping! In my town we have a quaint little downtown with tons of shop, almost all of which are individually owned (no large franchises). Since the bulk of my clients are small business owners, our downtown is a hub of potential new business.

I plan my shopping on weekdays, soon after the stores open when they are the least busy. I'm usually lucky enough to be the only customer in the store. While I'm shopping, I try and strike up a conversation with the sales person (who in the small stores is usually also the owner).

After we've developed some rapport, I begin talking to them about the services my company provides (web design and marketing). I always leave a business card, and if the conversation went well, I ask them if I can follow up with them on ways we might can help grow their business. Most often I get a yes and will follow up by phone a few days later.

This isn't a new tactic - as cold calling has been around for years... but rather than walking in and selling them myself... the process is much more casual and fun and when the conversation turns to business, it was a more natural flow of two people getting to know one another. They shop owner didn't feel as if they were being "sold", so they were much more receptive to what I had to say.

Oh, and the final trick... you have to buy something! Even if it's something super small and inexpensive, make sure you buy something. It's usually at the register that the conversation gets switched to business talk, and often I'm still chatting long after I've made my purchase. So not only is the shop owner in a more receptive place to listen to my pitch, I'm coming home happy too since I got to go shopping!"

Angela Nielsen
President/Creative Director,
One Lily Creative Agency, onelily.com

~ ACTION STEP ~

Write down right now what businesses or key people you would love to have as a new customer. Then go and build a relationship with them or someone in their organization and turn that cold call into a warm call.

36. Find Your Best Buyers

THIS MARKETING STRATEGY is so powerful that it could literally double or triple your business within a year – if you did nothing else!

I first learned this strategy from the amazing Chet Holmes who sadly passed away earlier this year. Chet was a master salesman and sales trainer and he studied his craft for years.

What he found was that most successful salespeople would do one of two things – focus on trying to sell customers who would be the easiest to close. Often these would be warm leads or contacts or smaller customers. But he found there was another strategy – to focus on selling only the customers who would bring in the biggest orders.

Chet called these the "best buyers." The best buyers will buy a massive amount of product and move it very quickly. For example, let's say you sell business insurance.

According to Chet, you should write down the top 50 best buyers who would buy the most amount of business insurance from you if they did buy. Then, you should focus 100% on selling these 50 people. If it takes you 5 years, so what? These are the 50 biggest buyers you will ever get for your business!

Even though it might be incredibly difficult to sell these 50 buyers, it will also be incredibly rewarding. Furthermore, because you ONLY have 50 potential clients (you've eliminated other potential clients from your mind), you've now got time to provide these customers with EXTREMELY exceptional service.

Instead of only having 1 hour to prepare for a sales presentation, you can afford to spend a week or even a month researching knowing that this customer is worth potentially millions to you and your business.

Instead of calling each potential customer once a month, you can call each potential customer once a week or even more often, providing more opportunities to educate the prospect and turn them into a happy customer.

36. FIND YOUR BEST BUYERS

~ **ACTION STEP** ~

Write down your "Best Buyers" list.

Don't write down who you think would be easy to sell – write down who you know would make the biggest purchase from you.

Don't stop until you have at least 20 Best Buyers on your list.

Then focus all your marketing efforts on these 20 Best Buyers.

37. Referral Program

IT'S SHOCKING TO me how few businesses actually have a formal referral program.

Let's get one thing straight right now – the only way you can run a truly profitable business is with word of mouth marketing. It is the most effective form of marketing in the world – and it's free!

Often, the real return from your marketing budget won't be due to the marketing you did – but to the word of mouth your prospects and customers did for you.

Every good salesperson knows to ask for referrals every time they make a sale – but few actually do it or create a system to do it effectively. You MUST create a referral system for your business!

What is a referral system?

The system could be anything from a set of steps every salesperson takes after they close a sale to a formal program with rewards and acknowledgements. One company I know of that has an incredible referral program is called Peak Potentials Training. The company provides business education seminars and workshops all over the world and it grew so fast thanks to its referral program.

The company pays each customer who refers a new customer 10% of all sales made. Not only that, but they have a formal name for it "The Ambassador Program" and they provide customers with free marketing materials to share the message – everything from brochures to manuals, pamphlets and even tickets to a free 3-day seminar to hand out!

Harv Eker, the founder of the company, told me that a huge part of their success was due to the word of mouth marketing generated by this referral program.

> **~ ACTION STEP ~**
>
> Create a referral program for YOUR business.
>
> You don't have to pay customers for referring new business to you but at least make it a system of ASKING them for referrals and following up with these referrals!

38. Networking

NETWORKING IS THE oldest marketing strategy in the world – and it's the ONLY necessary marketing strategy.

What do I mean by that?

Well, think about it – if you didn't have networking, how would you build relationships with new customers, business partners and investors? It would be almost impossible!

All successful entrepreneurs know how to network. It doesn't mean you have to network with every single person you ever meet (although some avid networkers do so). But it does mean you have to network with the right people in order to grow your contacts and your business.

Case Study

"While not necessarily unconventional, networking is still one of the most successful tools we've used to grow our business. Attending a networking event with intent and purpose can generate meaningful relationships. If several team members are attending the same event, a game can be created. See who can obtain the most business cards, but with a twist. Each card has to be signed by the person who's name is on the card. Not only does this keep networking entertaining, it also helps generate conversations with the people you meet.

Immediate follow up should also be a rule. Send a hand written note to each person you meet at the networking event. Keep it simple and sincere. Meetings will happen almost automatically."

Josh King,
virtualpeacock.com

> **~ ACTION STEP ~**
>
> Find a networking group you can join in your local area like BNI, a large international business networking and referrals organization.
>
> If you don't want to join a formal networking group then contact some people you already know and reconnect.
>
> Always remember that your success will be determined by the size and quality of your network.

39. Samples

EVERYONE LOVES FREE stuff! And trust me, it's a lot easier to get people to listen to you and your message and get out their credit cards to buy something after they've gotten something for free from you.

Case Study

"I started a small business in college selling products online. I realized early that our target demographic was college students.

I realized it was important for us to reach out to the community but to do so in a non-intrusive manner. We started to receive a lot of feedback from college students asking for free samples of our product, so we saw an opportunity.

We ended up launching a sponsorship program across hundreds of universities in the US and Canada. We sent them free samples, T-shirts, stickers, bags, etc.

They loved free product, and especially free gear, they would send us photo's of them wearing the gear, and using the product, and we used all of it to drive brand identity and loyalty initiatives.

It was gorilla marketing 101, but we were the first and only ones in our industry to do it. This initiative helped us grow by 20% in our first year."

Eugene Slobodetsky,
Opticsplanet.com

~ ACTION STEP ~

Find out where your target customers congregate and start giving away samples!

40. BE ENTERTAINING

THE AVERAGE AMERICAN spends over 4 hours a day watching TV and even more on the computer surfing the web. That's a lot of time the average person devotes to entertainment!

So if you want to market yourself "under the radar" so to speak, just entertain your customers!

Have you ever listened to a speaker who just bored you to death? Maybe they had amazing information to share that was incredibly valuable but they completely lacked humor and engagement. This is a class case of bad marketing – just pure information without entertainment.

The best form of marketing, by far, is marketing that is entertaining. Think of the Super Bowl commercials. Why do they get so much press? Why do companies spend millions of dollars on a single commercial? Why do all these companies compete for the "funniest" Super Bowl commercial? Because entertaining commercials lead to more sales!

Your customers and prospects will be far more receptive to your message if it's an interesting and entertaining message.

Case Study

"A few years back we had as our customer, mobile sales/repair store, Cellphone Doctor. It had no brand recognition and such stores were on every corner.

When opened its first branch in Russian Coney Island, we already had connections within the local sketch comedy scene. So, I put the manager/owners of the store on stage to perform live comedy as Cellphone Doctor, with corporate uniforms and jokes about cell phones. It worked well, with people laughing at the Cellphone Doctor guys, but remembering the brand associations."

David Kieve,
President, Double Speed Media,
2xspeed.me

~ ACTION STEP ~

Think of a way to entertain your customers, not just bombard them with advertising. You can do this offline or offline – and even incorporate entertainment in all of your marketing, depending on your brand.

Then launch your entertaining campaign and check the results!

41. Retail Partnerships

RETAIL PARTNERSHIPS CAN be a fantastic way to get your product in front of hundreds and even thousands of customers on a daily basis. A retail partnership is basically where you place your products for free in a business location. In exchange for the free use of your product, the business is giving you permission to market to their in-store traffic on a daily basis.

You can include brochures and marketing materials with your display or product, depending on what it is.

Case Study

"My start-up, DealDecor.com, sells furniture online, but we have an innovative offline marketing strategy. We've partnered with coffee shops to provide furniture samples for customers to view. Coffee shops get free furniture and customer traffic that we direct to their store.

We benefit by having a showroom without the overhead. 20% of our customers visited the coffee shop to see the sofa and many customers intended to see it, but just made the purchase because they ran out of time and trusted a company that put a sample in a public place. We're bridging the gap between ecommerce and brick and mortar business models with this marketing strategy."

Craig Sakuma,
DealDecor.com

~ ACTION STEP ~

Can you partner with other businesses to promote your products while at the same time providing them with free use of your product?

Call local business owners and see if they would like some free stuff! Who wouldn't?

42. Press Releases

PRESS RELEASES ARE powerful! They are one of the cheapest and easiest ways to get media contacts and massive exposure for your business.

All you need is: 1) a compelling story or "hook" as it's known in the business, 2) exposure and distribution and 3) a well-written release.

First, your hook is what makes your story relevant and important. For example, recently hurricane Sandy hit the North Eastern United States and every media outlet in the nation wants to publish any story they can think of related to the hurricane aftermath.

Did your business get affected by the hurricane? Did you have a dog who was lost in the hurricane? Pretty much anything related to the hurricane would get you on the news! Always be aware of what's current and hot right now in the media and it'll be easy to get exposure.

Second, you need exposure and distribution. You can get this with just about any press release service. For those of you on a budget, there are free press release options – just realize that you're sacrificing exposure.

Finally, you need a well-written press release. It should be compelling, clear and interesting. It should explain your hook immediately in the headline or first sentence. And it should be in the typical press release format (just research press releases out there and see how others do it if you're not sure how).

Case Study

"In the early days of CelebriDucks, I bought those big books of all the different media outlets and mailed out press releases myself. One day I got a call from a reporter at The Atlantic City Press. She said she got my press release and wanted to know why she should write about us. I thought about it for a moment and then told her that since I'm actually from New Jersey and used to go to Atlantic City all the time, why not??? So she says, "Ok".

The story appeared that weekend and the VP of the Philadelphia 76ers who lived in New Jersey happened to read it. He called me immediately and then flew out here to meet as he wanted us to do an Allen Iverson duck for a NBA promotion.

It was a huge hit! Then the Chicago Cubs, the Yankees, etc. all called and watnted to do promotions. We were all over ESPN and in the national media and before long I sold off the animation business and became all ducks

Also, the rubber duck was invented in America. Now they are all made overseas. We're bringing the whole industry back to the US this year and will be the only ones making them in America again!! You can read more about it on our website on the Made In America link on top. We expect a PR bonanza once we start sending out press releases about it in the coming month or two

For us, the key to becoming successful is finding what strikes a nerve in people and mobilizing their passion. Thus the Made in America is a really big deal. And we are gathering so much PR because we struck a different path from everyone else....much more expensive and stressful...but in the end...if you are the only ones doing something, you will build up a strong fan base and Facebook and Twitter today is a marketing Godsend for companies like us!

The humble press release has the power to change any company overnight!"

Craig Wolfe,
celebriducks.com

42. PRESS RELEASES

~ ACTION STEP ~

If you've never written a press release before, just Google recent press releases and learn from their style.

This is called R&D (Rip Off and Duplicate!).

Trust me, someone was paid way too much money to write that press release of a Fortune 500 company – so there's something you can learn from it.

If you're concerned about the cost of a press release, just use a free one for now.

You can use prlog.org to publish a free press release available online only. Although it will receive much less publicity, at least you will have gained the experience. And I've gotten several calls myself and new opportunities from publishing free press releases!

For premium paid press release distribution, I recommend prweb.com

43. Car Detailing and Logos

DO YOU HAVE a car or company cars? Why not get paid to drive them!

You can turn your car into a mobile marketing billboard for less than $200 with car decals, graphics and/or a vehicle wrap.

When I was 21 I decided to buy two large metallic car decals to promote my business with my website, phone number and some neat graphics. I spent $60 and received 6 new customers at an average customer lifetime value of $1,000, that's a nice payoff!

~ ACTION STEP ~

Are you comfortable turning your car into a mobile promotion for your business? If so, contact a local car graphics company and get an estimate and draw up some possible designs with them.

I only recommend this for a new or like-new car that you expect to drive for at least 3 years. It's not really attractive to take an old junker and put your website on it.

44. Coupons and Gift Vouchers

"I'M A FORMER retail toy store owner and a marketing consultant and drove traffic off-line by using a gift voucher.

At my toy store, we partnered up with local libraries, charities, and organizations to distribute $1 vouchers to our store (no strings attached, just an expiration date) for kids within the library programs or as reward incentives for those organizations.

The programs main purpose was to drive additional traffic by families whose children would want to redeem their "cash" for fun toys in our bins - we always kept them well stocked (and had many items at .99 price point) and it would drive large amounts of traffic to our retail location. Of course, children would come in with their parents who would be introduced to our store and purchase additional gifts and/or toys for their chidden.

Results over a three month period (June-August 2010) were over $8,000 in sales with a gross profit margin of 37.5% average ticket was closer to $25."

Aalap Shah,
SomeConnect.com

Another Story On Gift Cards

"Giving away gift cards has been a great way for us to introduce new customers to our business. Every day there are thousands of events that are open to potential gift card or goody bag sponsorship.

To make this work on a budget, we have issued such gift cards to have a value of $15.00. Considering that our average order value is $150, and we make on average, a 10% net margin, that allows us to give away the gift cards and attract new customers for free. By offering them great service we are able to retain the customer, and capitalize on their future value."

Justin Baynton,
Pink Taffy Designs,
pinktaffydesigns.com

> **~ ACTION STEP ~**
>
> Do the math! How much would someone need to buy to make your gift cards pay off?
>
> Remember to calculate the 10% to 20% of customers who will buy or receive gift cards and never redeem them.

45. Local Physical Marketing

WHEN YOUR CUSTOMERS walk around town, does your marketing reach them? If not, why not?

Every street corner, door handle and utility pole could be a chance to market your business (depending on the laws where you live). Don't be afraid to post fliers, door hangers and public signage to promote your products and services!

Case Study

"Expected approaches, and traditional advertising, are what people have gotten used to seeing. But that won't cut it anymore in an age of information overload. That's why it's essential to migrate approaches that work over into new and different sectors.

Case in point: door hangers.

It's not unusual to see door hangers for pizzerias or local restaurants. But we've had great success doing door-hanger campaigns for real estate projects and even municipalities. During the depths of the real-estate collapse, we were able to sell out an entire condo project with a door hanger campaign.

And in working with the City of Santa Monica, which was looking for new ways to communicate the range of city services available to residents, we were able to do a door hanger distribution that generated widespread attention within the city."

Lee Wochner,
CEO and Chief Strategist for
COUNTERINTUITY Creative Marketing,
counterintuity.com

~ ACTION STEPS ~

Walk around your town and see if there's any local signage, fliers, door hangers or other physical marketing pieces around.
Experiment with different strategies and see what works for your business in your city.

46. Donating Books

"WE RESELL A book on our website called *Living Clay*. We are not the author but it is a great resource for people to learn about how they can use calcium bentonite clay in their daily lives. We have a book donation program where anyone (doesn't have to be a customer) can request that we donate a copy to their local library.

We simply ask that they provide us with the name and contact info of the Circulation Manager or other person that handles book donations. We then contact the library about donating the book.

We put a book plate in the front cover of the book (attached) so that patrons know about us and our gift. This is an important strategy to use because an important part of our mission is to educate the mainstream market about the benefits of calcium bentonite clay. And in this tough economy, not everyone can afford to buy books!"

Janet Lancaster,
earthslivingclay.com

47. Gift Bags

GIFT BAGS ARE used all the time in marketing, especially when it comes to celebrity and red carpet events. But your customers don't have to be celebrities for gift bags to pay off (and you don't need to know any celebrities to put this strategy into action).

Again, customers love free stuff – and gift bags are no exception. But you can't afford to just give out a gift bag to everyone in the world – so you need to select your target market wisely and choose whom to give the bags to.

Case Study

"As a new mortgage loan officer, I didn't have a lot of money to play with and I needed to get my name out ASAP. I came up with two strategies and they both worked very well.

First, I bought premium dog treats, wrapped them in cellophane and tied them with a ribbon to a flyer, which read: "Everyone and their dog can promise on-time closings. But we're the only ones closing loans in eight days!" Realtors in this area are hugely into dogs - they sponsor all kinds of fund-raisers for our shelters, etc. and I got lots of positive feedback and some new agents.

Second, I didn't have a huge budget for taking folks out to lunch, and I hit upon this way to take lots of people to lunch. I found companies that had just moved to Reno, like Cisco Systems. I bought some bright red bags (exactly matching the color of my company's logo). I filled them with bottled water, energy bars, small apples, packets of nuts, etc., and stapled a note and my business card/ The note read, "If you work through lunch as often as I do, you need this." If you're looking for the best mortgage financing, you need me!"

My strategy centered on two things - knowing my target (real estate agents who love dogs, and new residents with jobs), and finding a way to stand out.. I'm currently a senior marketing manager with LendingTree. My degrees are in financial management and accounting, but it was my "real-world" training that got me successfully into the fabulous job that I have now."

Gina L. Pogol,
LendingTree.com

> **~ ACTION STEP ~**
>
> Who is your target market?
>
> Could you create a unique gift bag or basket to give to your target customers to attract some new customers really quickly?

47. Fundraising For Charity

RAISING MONEY FOR charity isn't just a good thing to do, it's also good business. That's why just about every Fortune 500 not only donates a lot of money to charity, but also publicizes their charity efforts.

Big businesses understand the power of a charity-driven mission or event – but few small business owners do! Just one annual event in your area for charity could dramatically increase your business and attract new deals and opportunities you could have never found elsewhere. Not to mention all the free publicity you'll be getting!

Case Study

"This is a new strategy for us that dovetails with our online affiliate program. We recently introduced a line of veterinarian-endorsed pet products to the market that feature calcium bentonite clay.

We partner with animal rescue organizations on their adoption events and setup a table with our products at the event. We educate pet lovers about our products and 15% of all sales at the event are donated to the rescue organization. (The online feature of our affiliate program is traditional where companies and organizations can post one of our banners on their website. When a visitor to their site clicks through and purchases, our shopping cart tracks that user's purchase and we payout 15% of the sales to the affiliate.)"

Janet Lancaster,
earthslivingclay.com

~ ACTION STEPS ~

Are you passionate about a cause or charity? If so, contact them and see how you can support them.

If you have the resources, ask them to help you host an event to raise money for them (no charity would say no!).

If not, at least you can partner with them in smaller ways. You can, for example, add a banner of the charity's logo to your website – giving you more credibility and helping the charity as well.

Studies have shown that websites with charity banners convert more visitors into customers and deepen trust.

If you've been successful as an entrepreneur, you have a huge opportunity to help others and help grow your business at the same time.

Don't pass it up! Life is too short not to give to a worthy cause.

48. Write a Thank You Note

IT'S BEEN FASCINATING for me to watch as the internet revolution has changed everything from how we communicate to how we do business. Email took over mail and what used to be the fine art of hand-written notes has all but faded away.

But there are still a few old fashioned entrepreneurs and sales people who write hand-written notes and have great success with it.

Think about it – how many hand-written notes have you received in the last year? I'm guessing you could count them with your fingers.

How many emails have you received in the last year? Too many to count!

A basic principle of human psychology and economics is that anything that is scarce is more valuable and anything that is abundant becomes less valuable. Sure, sending a thank you email is still important and you should do it. But why not send a hand-written thank you note as well?

Trust me, your competition isn't doing this. And anything you can do differently will set you apart.

Of course, this strategy might not be practical if you sell a $5 product – it's probably not worth the time let alone the postage to send a hand-written thank you note to every $5 customer.

But what about your distributors? What about your wholesale customers? I know there are people in your business whom you depend on – so why not let them know you appreciate the work they do for you?

Sometimes the best marketing isn't about finding new customers or partnerships – it's about keeping the ones you have.

~ ACTION STEP ~

Write down on a piece of paper the 5 most important people in your business right now.

Maybe it's your biggest customer, a distributor, business partner or key employee.

Write them a thank-you note and deliver it ASAP.

Always remember the credo:

"Long term relationships lead to long-term business success."

49. Community Classes

FEW THINGS WILL bring you closer to potential customers than getting in front of a room of people who are eager to learn what you know. That's exactly what you can do by teaching a community class!

You can either teach a regular weekly class or just small workshops here and there. You can charge for the classes or make them free. The key here is to get butts in seats in front of you (or someone in your organization) who can teach the public something they're interested in.

Case Study

"On a national level, writing my book has given me many more opportunities. We've done advertising too, of course, but locally the best method has been to have a business presence in related fields or complementary settings. I mean that not only in the complementary alternative medicine framework that is our business but in overlapping fields of expertise.

For instance, I teach classes on nutrition and found that alternating venues between various health food stores and the chiropractor's office where I do consults helped attract different clientele. The gluten-free catering side of the business is the most time-consuming but meshes well with my more hands-on classes and attracts clients from area restaurants.

Although it saves on advertising costs, the major risk of this approach is spreading myself too thin and not whole concentrating on one specific service we provide. So far, strategically planning what I do geographically has helped grow the business, but I have to be careful not to over-diversify and confuse people about what all I do."

Melanie Angelis, BSEd, MS CAM,
thegreciangarden.com

~ ACTION STEPS ~

Contact your local colleges, newspapers and any local education programs and see if you might be able to teach a community class there.

50. Postcards For Local Businesses

"I AM AN entrepreneur and my first business is a dog nanny service serving Manhattan and Queens. I received about 10% of clients from printing postcards and distributing them to local businesses. I would say that the most referrals came from Dry Cleaning places.

The reason I believe this works is because people are not necessarily looking for certain flyers and things when they are at other businesses, but when they do see them, they take them. I would give a brief into about myself and ask if they would keep a stack of flyers (5-8).

The second off line method that I used was to volunteer and have booths at a lot of pet events. Businesses can do this in their respective industries.

I would give away a free service, get to know the participants at the events and collect their information and follow-up later. People already stopping by at your booth are interested, so it's just a matter or genuinely connecting and building a relationship.

Partnering with businesses that provide non-competing services is another great idea. I have a good relationship with the local pet store, dog walkers in the area and the vet. Everyone is providing non-competing goods/services and helps with cross-referalls. It's obviously important to make sure you connect with them and you fully can 100% back their recommendations and services."

Cynthia Okimoto,
New York Dog Nanny,
newyorkdognanny.com

51. Create A Controversial Policy

CREATING A CONTROVERSIAL policy can be a great way to get free publicity and generate a huge increase in sales. In his book *The Adweek Copywriting Handbook*, Joseph Sugarman, renowned copywriter, shares an amazing story about how effective this strategy can be.

Joseph tells a story of a client who owned a snow mobile company. Well, they came up with this crazy idea to create a policy NOT to sell snow mobiles to any women because it was "too dangerous." Then they published it in a press release and the media went into a frenzy debating the sexism of this policy.

Well, snow mobile sales shot up instantly overnight and two weeks later the company withdrew the policy and released a new press release saying that they were creating a training program to teach women how to ride safely.

Afterwards, snow mobile sales increased dramatically for both men and women and the training program was a big hit as well.

~ ACTION STEP ~

Can you add a little controversy to your business to create a media frenzy?

Even negative publicity can help your business generate a lot of new business – and with a company policy, you can always change it later.

Just make sure to consult your attorney so that you don't get sued for discrimination or breaking any other laws.

52. Create A Documentary

WHEN I LIVED in Indiana, I went to a business networking group and one of the speakers was sharing his story of how his company came to be featured in a full-length documentary. The man owned a very small, custom metal manufacturing company. They made all kinds of custom metal license plates, tags and other weird metal memorabilia (like metal books).

So he came up with this idea to build a metal book memorializing all the people who lose their lives in 9/11. Word got around with what he was doing, the media picked it up and a documentary film producer contacted him and asked if he wanted to do a documentary about creating the memorial and delivering it to Ground Zero.

I thought this was an ingenious way for this tiny little Indiana metal manufacturer to get some great national publicity – all for the cost of just making a little memorial metal book and the time spent in the process. But he didn't do it just to get publicity – he honestly wanted to help and create something special that would touch and improve peoeple's lives. This just goes to show that you can do good for others and succeed in business at the same time.

> **~ ACTION STEP ~**
>
> What can you do for your community or country to help and make a difference?
>
> Is there a cause bigger than yourself or your company that you can create something unique for or devote time, effort or money towards?
>
> You too can be featured in a documentary!

53. Direct Mail

DIRECT MAIL USED to be the most commonly used form of marketing, especially for sales people. Today, though, it's very rarely used.

The only marketing mail I get nowadays is from credit card companies pretty much. Yet I get over 100 emails a day!

Do you think you'd have a better chance of reaching me by sending me 1 out of 100 emails or by sending me the only legitimate piece of mail I receive today? You have a much better chance using snail mail!

Make It Personal!

The biggest problem with snail mail solicitations today is that they all look like junk mail! It's so obvious when the postage is pre-paid and the address is written by a computer printer instead of a human's penmanship.

If you want me (or your customer) to read your mail, make it personal! Make the address and return address hand-written. Use a stamp – more than one stamp is even better!

Don't put the name of your company on the outside of the envelope – you don't want to give away who it's from!

Also try to get unique looking envelopes – different shapes, sizes and colors instead of the standard white manila envelope.

WHERE TO GET YOUR MAILING LIST

In direct mail, the mailing list you use will determine your success. If you have a good list, you will likely have success. If you have a poor list, you'll probably just be throwing your money away.

How do you get a good list? Well, the best list you can ever use is your list of current and past customers! Think about it – they already know you and you already know them. It's also free because you've already got the list in your database (you do keep good customer records right?).

> **~ ACTION STEP ~**
>
> Go back through your customer records and create one or several new mailing lists based on their location, buying habits and other important information you have.
>
> Then start your current and past customers on your mailing campaign and measure the results.
>
> If you can't turn a profit mailing to your past customers then don't bother buying a mailing list from somewhere else!

54. Flyers

FLYERS CAN BE such a powerful way to market locally.

Tips For Posting Flyers

Always print in color and use bright colors in your design. This makes your flyer stand out and attract more attention and eyeballs.

Always include tear-off tabs at the bottom of your flyers with contact/RSVP info – this allows multiple leads to come from that one flyer – otherwise people will either take the flyer and no one else will see it or they won't take it and will forget all about it.

You can post flyers at most grocery stores, health food stores, gyms, libraries, community buildings, college campuses and just about anywhere else you can think of – use your creativity!

~ ACTION STEP ~

Create a flyer to promote a local marketing event or just promote your products and services to the community.

Carry them with you in your car and when you notice a posting board or kiosk with flyers.

55. Handing Out Branded Apparel

GIVING OUT BRANDED apparel can be a great way to get more exposure especially in a local or niche market. For example, credit card companies will often hand out branded t-shirts and wrist bands on college campuses, either for free or in return for applying for a credit card.

When you do hand out branded apparel, though, it should be an "event" not just giving away free stuff. It should be fun, engaging and allow for conversations with customers and sales. You should have salespeople there who are trained to sign up customers, not just people who hand out a t-shirt and then start texting their friends and ignore the customers.

56. Create A Business Marketing Research Project

CONDUCTING A RESEARCH study can be an incredible way to connect with prospects and convert them into customers. I remember one retail chain when I was a teenager where the employees would stand outside the store. When a young person like me walked by, they would ask if I was interested in taking their survey.

In the survey, they asked me questions about my taste in clothes and fashion and then showed me some of their new clothes for the season. Before the survey was over, they were asking me if I wanted to buy clothes!

Although I was put off at the time by this marketing tactic, I've since found that it is incredibly powerful – and can be done ethically and in good taste as well. Think about it – what kind of information do your customers want and how can you get it for them or show it to them?

For example, if you sell sunglasses you could do a "sunglass study" and have people try on your sunglasses for free for a few minutes and see if their eyes feel better. It may sound silly at first, but doing research like this is an invaluable way to connect with prospects and help them see the value in your products.

This marketing strategy is so powerful and effective because it uses the reciprocity urge that is in all our DNA. Humans naturally want to reciprocate a gift. And giving someone information or a free test drive of your product makes them want to do something to return the favor – like buy from you!

CASE STUDY

"I work with interns every summer to help them get real life experience. Recently, I worked with an intern and provided 8 prospects and 2 customers with a $100 credit to try out pay-per-click advertising. Google supplied the credits and I shared these credits with targeted business owners from different industries. The industries represented in this study included insurance, photography, restaurant, floral, accounting, retail, publishing, and consulting.

The goals of the study for me and my business were to build and develop relationships with key prospects and customers and demonstrate my capabilities in marketing strategy. In addition, my philosophy is to always add value where possible to the people I work with. Finally I embrace the opportunity to provide real life experience for interns to help differentiate them from other candidates in this very competitive job market.

The business goals of this study were to help business people understand pay-per-click advertising and determine if this would be an effective marketing technique for his or her business. The participants' individual goals included to increase website traffic, increase visibility with their target market, increase sales and grow their lead lists.

Each participant was provided with an internet marketing guide that we created to help them ensure they would best optimize their ad credits. This guide assisted them in establishing online advertising goals, creating ad copy and identifying appropriate keywords for attracting the right people that fit their target market criteria. We also provided information about how to optimize their landing page so when people click on their ads, they have a positive experience with a very specific call to action to encourage sales.

We reviewed each ad and landing page and provided custom recommendations to each participant since industry differences will impact the bid prices for key words and there will be different messaging requirements needed based on target market needs. Recommendations included references to topics such as:

Create a catchier title to grab attention.

Include references to specific locations if businesses serviced particular geographic locations.

Include a specific call to action like to download a whitepaper, access to a special promotion, to click on a "buy now" button etc.

Ads should have information to differentiate businesses from competitors.

Messages need to be concise.

Pictures can be included to draw attention to the ad.

Testimonials can be used to establish credibility.

Examples of work can be shown to demonstrate capabilities.

Align landing page copy with ad message to ensure consistency.

Landing page should be organized for easy viewing and navigation.

As a result of this project, all participants reported an increase in leads and three businesses generated a direct sale as a result of using Google ads with the free ad credit during this three week period.

I believe marketing is about developing meaningful and profitable relationships and providing this study allowed me to provide value to my customers and prospects and enabled me to form closer relationships resulting in 75% conversion rate of my prospects to customers."

Sheryl Johnson,
Founder BD-PRo Marketing Solutions,
bdpromarketing.com

~ ACTION STEP ~

Write down what kind of research project you can create to connect with your customers.

What resources would you need to create a project?

57. Radio and Media Appearances

RADIO IS ONE of the most powerful marketing strategies on the planet!

Even though radio, television and newspapers are in a general decline or at least certainly not growing as fast as the internet, millions of people still tune in to the radio every day. And a simple 5, 15 or 60 minute radio interview could generate thousands of leads for your business!

But how do you go about getting booked on a radio show? Well, you can always hire a PR firm. If you do, expect to pay at least $1,000 a month. High quality PR firms often charge around $5,000 a month.

But there are much more cost effective ways to get media interviews if you're willing to invest the time.

One great way is to use free services like Help A Reporter Out (HARO), Reporter Connection and PitchRate. You can sign up for the daily leads from reporters, journalists and the media looking to interview or get quotes from experts like you. Regardless of your business or background, I guarantee you'll find valuable media connections using these services – and it's all free! It just takes a few minutes of time each day to go through the pitches and see what's a good fit for you.

You can sign up for these free services online at .

Helpareporter.com

pitchrate.com

and

reporterconnection.com

Bonus Marketing Tips

Fifty-seven marketing strategies just wasn't enough! We had to share a few more. In business, you should always go the extra mile. Don't give up when you think you're done – keep going and you'll often find your best marketing ideas come after you thought you were done!

Promoting Your Website Offline

"AS A BLOGGER, I've become very adept at promoting myself online. This summer, I decided to start promoting myself locally and my methods worked. It's increased local traffic, I'm recognized in my community, and I've made some fabulous local connections.

1. Turn your car into your bill board: I put Keep the Tail Wagging on my rear window and now look forward to traffic!
2. Attend local festivals and events. I sponsored two this summer, handed out business cards, helpful tips for dog lovers on saving money, helpful tips for business owners to promote their brand, and I raffled off a gift basket. Worth every penny and I

didn't spend much – less than $300 for the entire summer.

3. Attach business cards/flyers on neighborhood cork boards; I chose local teriyaki joints, the Co Op, local veterinarian offices, and the churches.

One day I was walking to my car after grocery shopping and someone approached me and thanked me for my blog and said they loved it. I'm always approached at the local dog park by fellow dog owners. It's a blast. Great for my traffic and fantastic for advertisers on my site. Best of luck with your article. Please let me know if you need more information."

Kimberly,
keepthetailwagging.com

Tracking Phone Calls From Your Website

"THE MAJORITY OF our clients are business-to-business companies, and many of their sales with hefty price tags still happen over the phone.

In fact, for B2B, studies have shown that close to 70% of a website's conversions take place via phone calls. We've taken this into consideration and have integrated offline call tracking into our behavioral analysis. Call tracking closes the marketing loop - our clients see what advertising expenditures are generating leads. We listen to the phone calls and assess the quality of the leads as well as the quality of the clients' customer service. We can also discover ways to improve the content of a site based on real-time customer feedback. In addition, evaluating the overall phone call recording can shed light into the quality of the opportunity and how a client's team is managing these opportunities.

Not tracking phone calls as part of website performance can be detrimental.

Here's a video showing our call tracking solution and how it integrates with our reporting:

youtu.be/RRpLSAikZnA."

Nicole Buergers,
topspotims.com

Bonus Sales Tip

MARKETING IS ONE thing but sales is another! Marketing will get people in the door or on the phone but sometimes you need to close a sale in person. Here's some great advice on how to do just that.

The 3 Step Sales Rejection Rule

"The 3 Step Sales Rejection Rule is guaranteed to increase your sales!

When starting out doing any form of selling we tend to let the customer take control of the situation. NOW ITS YOUR TURN TO TAKE CONTROL! How many times have you seen this scenario play out:

> SALES PERSON: Hello would you like to buy this <PRODUCT HERE>?
>
> CUSTOMER: No thanks.

SALES PERSON: Ok, no problem.

Notice anything? The difference between a seasoned sales person and a brand new sales person is that a seasoned sales person does not just stop at the first rejection! You will notice that you will close more sales if you are able to take on 3 specific rejections, hence the 3 Step Sales Rejection Rule!

After the first rejection, ask "WHY NOT?" attaching a quick benefit of the product related to the customer. "Why Not" puts the ball in the customers court to really think of a reason to reject your product and attaching a benefit gives them a chance of thinking about how they themselves would be using it. At this point they have to think fast and come up with what we call a barrier that is between you and closing the deal. This specific barrier could be related to budget, but in many cases it has to do with other factors such as time, space or other specific factors. This first rejection should be something that gets the customer thinking and really opens up the sales conversation!

Here is the conversation again with the first rejection and a proper response using the 3 Step Sales Rejection Rule (3SSRR or TRESSER as I like to call it):

SALES PERSON: Hello would you like to buy this <PRODUCT HERE>?

CUSTOMER (FEMALE): No Thanks (rejection one)

SALES PERSON: Why not? It's shiny and cute and can easily fit into your purse.

CUSTOMER (FEMALE): Hmm sounds interesting...(After a little bit of thought) I'll pass (rejection two)

Ok so now as you can see I've shown you how we have now successfully got to rejection 2. A small handful of purchasers close the deal after the first rejection "WHY NOT". MOST others close the deal after overcoming the second rejection. The second rejection (As seen above) requires showing the customer in a visual way how the product/service will benefit them or by helping build their own visualization of THEM actually using the product. Also always remember COMPLIMENTS ARE FREE, USE THEM OFTEN!

Here is the TRESSER conversation again but this time overcoming the second rejection (Remember after doing this successfully many people end up closing in on the deal):

SALES PERSON: Hello would you like to buy this <PRODUCT HERE>?

CUSTOMER (FEMALE): No Thanks

SALES PERSON: Why not? It's shiny and cute and can easily fit into your purse.

CUSTOMER (FEMALE): Hmm sounds interesting...(After a little bit of thought) I'll pass (rejection two)

> SALES PERSON: Ok before you go just try it out, here hold it in your hand (Passes it to customer, now customer is actually using the product). See how it glistens and sparkles? It adds to your already existing beauty and even comes in a variety of colors! Do you like Gold or Silver?
>
> CUSTOMER (FEMALE): Gold
>
> SALES PERSON: Ah of course! Gold is a great color and matches your purse perfectly. See, it definitely suits you!

At this point more than likely you have a closed deal, however if a customer does end up saying no a final time (hence the 3rd rejection) you thank them and let them go at that point. If you do this technique with EVERY customer EVERY time, you will see a major difference in sales numbers!

When I started implementing this method of sales, I was able to increase my sales volume by 1000%! I went from selling 1 unit of a service package to over 10 packages a day even when the average sales person was bringing in 0 to 2 packages a day! I was doing 10 using this method and now you can use the same method too!

The 3 Step Sales Rejection Rule, or TRESSER for short, is a KILLER sales tool that will help you to increase your sales!"

Abhinav Gupta,
CEO, gamescorpion.com

SPECIAL FACEBOOK GROUP

COME JOIN OUR Facebook group just for readers like you who want to take their marketing to the next level. In this group we'll be sharing our successes, marketing tips and strategies with each other so that we can all continue to grow our businesses together.

This is also a fantastic group for finding joint venture partners and cross-promotion opportunities! Imagine if you had hundreds of other entrepreneurs from all over the world collaborating with you – imagine how big of an impact you could have.

It's also a great place to get any marketing questions you have answered as well.

Come join us here on Facebook:

www.faceBook.com/groups/EntrepreneurSuccessGroup

FREE BLOGGING FOR BUSINESS TRAINING

If you're a business owner and want to learn how to start a blog for your business that makes a profit, I've developed a free online training program to teach you everything from how to build your blog to getting traffic to monetizing it.

You can get the free training at:

www.BlogBusinessSchool.com

Connect With The Author

THANK YOU SO much for taking the time to read this book. I'm excited for you to start your path to making the income of your dreams using these marketing strategies.

If you have any questions of any kind, feel free to contact me at:

    www.tckpublishing.com/contact

You can follow me on Twitter:

    @JuiceTom

And connect with me on Facebook:

    www.tckpublishing.com/faceBook

You can check out my publishing blog for the latest updates here:

www.TCKpublishing.com

I'm wishing you the best of health, happiness and success!

Here's to you!

Tom Corson-Knowles

About The Author

TOM CORSON-KNOWLES is the #1 Amazon best-selling author of *The Kindle Publishing Bible* and *How To Make Money With Twitter*, among others. He lives in Kapaa, Hawaii. Tom loves educating and inspiring other entrepreneurs to succeed and live their dreams.

Learn more at:
http://Amazon.com/author/business

Get Tom's free newsletter for more marketing tips at:
www.BlogBusinessSchool.com

OTHER BOOKS BY TOM CORSON-KNOWLES

Destroy Your Distractions

Email Marketing Mastery

The Book Marketing Bible

Schedule Your Success

You Can't Cheat Success! How The Little Things You Think Aren't Important Are The Most Important of All

Guest Blogging Goldmine

Rules of the Rich: 28 Proven Strategies for Creating a Healthy, Wealthy and Happy Life and Escapign the Rat Race Once and For All

Systemize, Automate, Delegate: How To Grow A Business While Traveling, On Vacation And Taking Time Off

The Kindle Publishing Bible: How To Sell More Kindle Ebooks On Amazon

How To Make Money With Twitter

101 Ways To Start A Business For Less Than $1,000

Facebook For Business Owners: Facebook Marketing For Fan Page Owners And Small Businesses

How To Reduce Your Debt Overnight: A Simple System To Eliminate Credit Card And Consumer Debt

The Network Marketing Manual: Work From Home And Get Rich In Direct Sales

Index

A

affiliate marketing.........18–19
Alexa Rank...............32–33, 64
American Airlines................85
Angelis, Melanie................141
article writing......................55
Audacity [software].............24

B

backlinks........................50, 51
Baynton, Justin..................125
Blogging
    Alexa Rank................32–33
    guest.........................27–40
    product reviews.......63–64
    self-hosted................25–26

Blogging cont/d:
    Tomoson........................63
    training.........................172
BNI.....................................110
books, donating...........129–30
Branding
    apparel.........................153
    products...................93–96
Buergers, Nicole................165
business cards...............72–75
Butler, Nancy D...................99
buyers, best...................103–5

C

call tracking.................164–65

Camtasia [software] 24
car detailing & logos ... 122–23
Case Studies:
 branded product 93–95
 cold calling 101–2
 community classes. 140–41
 coupon sites 73–74
 coupons & gift
  vouchers 124–25
 customer marketing 88–90
 entertaining marketing 114
 fundraising 135
 gift bags 131–32
 LinkedIn 11–12
 local marketing 127–28
 networking 109
 postcards 142–43
 press releases 119–20
 public speaking 97–98
 research studies..... 155–58
 retail partnerships . 116–17
 samples 111–12
 writing a book 82–83
charities 91
charity fundraising 134–36
classes, community 140–41
cold calling 100–102
community service
 See volunteering
controversy 144–45
coupon sites 65–67

coupons/gift vouchers 124–25
Craigslist 43, 55, 57
customer marketing 88–90

D

demographic, female 14
direct mail 148–50
documentary-making . 146–47
Dyer, Dr. Samuel 98

E

eBook publishing 41–43
Eker, Harv 107
entertaining marketing 113–14
events 91–92
EzineArticles 55

F

Facebook:
 ads 44–45
 entrepreneurs group ... 171
 fan pages 3–5
 -Offers 67
Fiverr 50
flyers 151–52
Fortune 500 ..... 8, 85, 121, 134
forums, niche 16–17
fundraising 134–36

G

gift bags 131–33
gift vouchers
   See coupons & gift
   vouchers
GoArticles............................55
GoDaddy 75
Google:
   AdSense..........................33
   AdWords 44–45
   PageRank............31–32, 64
Google Hangouts............23, 24
Groupon 65
Groups:
   Facebook 171
   LinkedIn..........................10
Gupta, Abhinav 170

H

HARO (Help A Reporter
   Out) 160
Holmes, Chet.....................103
*How To Make Money With
   Twitter* 9

I

iTunes............................22, 23

J

Johnson, Sheryl 158
joint ventures................20–21

K

keywords.....................51, 156
Kieve, David.......................114
Kindle 42, 175, 178
King, Josh 109

L

Lancaster, Janet 130, 135
libraries 99, 124, 151
LinkedIn........................10–13

M

mailing lists 149, 150
marketing, local 127–28
McFadden, Patrick 90
MeetUp........................68–70
membership site/
   program...................60–62
Mountain Dew 56

N

Netflix............................18, 61
networking..................108–10
Nielsen, Angela 102

O

offline website promotion 162–63
Okimoto, Cynthia 143

P

Peak Potentials Training ... 107
phone calls 84–87
phone calls, tracking ... 164–65
Pinerly 15
Pinterest 14–15
PitchRate 160
Pogol, Gina L. 132
postcards 142–43
PPC (pay-per-click) ads . 44–45
press releases 118–21
product reviews 63–64
public speaking 97–99

R

R&D (rip off & duplicate) .. 121
radio/media appearances 159–60
Rasiej, John 83
referral program 106–7
referrals 8, 107, 142
rejection, 3 step rule .. 167–70
report, free 52–54
Reporter Connection 160
research studies 154–58

retail partnerships 116–17

S

Sakuma, Craig 117
sales tip 167–70
samples 111–12
SBA (Small Business Mentoring Program) 80–81
Screenflow [software] 24
SEO (search engine optimization) 50–51
Shah, Aalap 125
Slobodetsky, Eugene 112
song writing 56–57
Squidoo 46–47
Sugarman, Joseph 144

T

telephone calls 84–87
Toastmasters 98
Twitter 8–9, 85

V

video marketing 48–49
Vistaprint 73
volunteering 78–79

W

Wochner, Lee 128

Wolfe, Craig 120
WordPress:
   affiliate plugins 19
   guest blogging 35
   podcasting plugin 23
Writing:
   articles 55
   books 82–83
   newspapers/
      magazines 76–77

songs 56–57
thank you notes 137–39

Y

YouTube 6–7

Z

Zappos 48

www.ingramcontent.com/pod-product-compliance
Lightning Source LLC
Chambersburg PA
CBHW052028070526
44584CB00016B/1953